River Cafe
Italian Kitchen
Rose Gray and Ruth Rogers

Ebury Press • London

River Cafe
Italian Kitchen

Photography: Neville Kidd Text and recipe assistants: Lucy Boyd and Alex Colman Design: the Senate

First published in 1998   5 7 9 10 8 6   Text copyright © Rose Gray and Ruth Rogers 1998 All rights reserved. No part of this publi-cation may be reproduced, stored in a retrieval system, or transmitted in any form or by any means, electronic, mechanical, photocopying, recording or otherwise, without the prior permission of the copyright owners. Ruth Rogers and Rose Gray have asserted their right to be identified as authors of this work. First published in 1998 by Ebury Press, Random House, 20 Vauxhall Bridge Road, London SW1V 2SA. Random House Australia (Pty) Limited, 20 Alfred Street, Milsons Point, Sydney, New South Wales 2061, Australia. Random House New Zealand Limited, 18 Poland Road, Glenfield, Auckland 10, New Zealand. **Random House (Pty) Limited, Isle of Houghton, Corner of Boundary Road & Carse O'Gowrie Houghton 2198, South Africa** Random House Group Limited Reg. No. 954009. A CIP catalogue record for this book is available from the British Library.
ISBN 9780091867980 (from Jan 2007), ISBN 0091867983
Printed and bound in China by Midas Printing International Ltd.

Contents

The food we cook in *The Italian Kitchen*, like the food we cook in the River Cafe, is inspired by the seasons – late spring and early summer in series one and autumn and early winter in series two.

We want you to be as excited as we are by the variety of vegetables and other produce which are particular to these seasons and learn as we did to use basil in the summer when the flavour is pungent, make polenta in the autumn when the maize has just been milled, and cook fennel in the winter before the bulbs start to shoot and into tough stalks.

All the recipes we cook in the programmes can be cooked at home. We demonstrate the techniques we use in the restaurant, and work with alternative equipment – griddle pans instead of the char-grill and domestic ovens at high heat instead of the wood oven. In every programme there are simple recipes with few ingredients that can be prepared quickly such as Spaghetti al Limone as well as demanding ones such as Bollito Misto – but all the recipes represent what is, to us, the essence of Italian food.

The photographs in this book are of the people who make the Parmesan, find the truffles, produce the wine and press the olives. Their care and precision, their passion and knowledge inspire us. We want, through this book, and the television series, to inspire you to cook these recipes, to get pleasure from using such special ingredients and to feel more confident and knowledgeable about cooking Italian food, the food we love most.

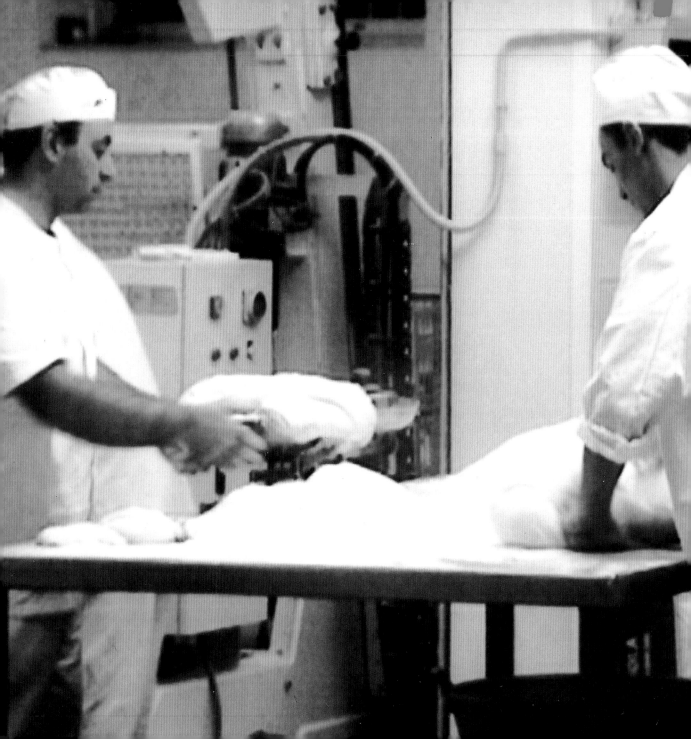

Soups

The Italian soups we cook have been chosen not only because they are the ones we like most but because they convey our approach to cooking so well. They are robust and thick and are often served as an alternative to risotto or pasta.

We have picked soups that reflect both the different regions and seasons. Broth soups from North Italy, like Risi Bisi Verde, a soupy risotto made only in the early summer with peas, spinach, rice and Parmesan; bread soups like Summer Ribollita, thickened with fresh cannellini beans and seasoned with summer herbs; and the famous very, very simple Pappa al Pomodoro which has only four ingredients and is so regional that you would hardly find it outside Tuscany. From Puglia in the south of Italy we chose to make our favourite fish soup – Spicy Mussel Soup – the key ingredients being tomatoes and fiery chilli.

In the autumn series we show you how to make Pumpkin, Chestnut and Farro Soup. These ingredients are all harvested, and are at their best, from October to December. In Tuscany, in the first week of November, the pressing of the new season's olive oil starts. This oil has a very special, intensely peppery flavour and gives us the perfect reason to make Cannellini Bean and Parsley Soup.

We hope that making these soups with their distinctive

characteristics will inspire you to adopt our approach to ingredients, choosing them with real care and preparing them in a precise and exciting way.

Summer Ribollita (see page 16)

The word 'ribollita' means 're-boiled', and traditionally was applied to leftover minestrone which was reheated on the second day and served with added bread. The classic ribollita is made with dried beans and cavolo nero, a winter vegetable. Our summer ribollita uses fresh cannellini beans, Swiss chard and summer herbs.

The soffritto forms the base of the soup. Onions, celery, chard stalks and herbs are cooked together gently for the soffritto which is particularly important to the taste as there is no stock to enrich the flavour. The best extra virgin olive oil is an essential ingredient.

Tuscan Bread, Tomato and Basil Soup (see page 18)

This simple, thick soup is found only in Tuscany, where there are almost as many local versions as there are local cooks. Every small trattoria will have Pappa al Pomodoro on the menu, especially in late summer when tomatoes and basil are at their best. Our version relies on really ripe and flavourful tomatoes (although good-quality tinned can be substituted), the pungency of fresh basil, summer garlic and extra virgin olive oil. The bread used must have strength, and should ideally be a sourdough bread such as ciabatta or Pugliese, both of which are made with olive oil.

Chestnut, Pumpkin and Farro Soup (see page 20)

Made only in October and November (when chestnuts and pumpkins are in season) this is a typical River Cafe soup. The flavour comes from the chestnuts which are very sweet, and the pumpkin which is roasted to concentrate the taste. The first two ingredients are soft and floury, so the farro, which is soaked and cooked separately, is added to give texture.

Chicken Broth (see page 22)

The best chickens to use when making stocks are free-range boilers. This stock should taste of chicken rather than vegetables and herbs; simply use carrots, onions and celery, keeping both the chicken and the vegetables whole. It is cooked for less time than the more traditional methods in order to achieve a lighter stock.

Fish Broth (see page 23)

Use turbot bones and halibut and monkfish trimmings to make this fish stock. Put them with herbs and vegetables which complement fish – for example, bay, fennel and fennel seeds, chillies and parsley stalks. White wine or dry vermouth adds perfume and depth to the stock. Cook the ingredients gently for only 20 minutes.

Asparagus Broth with Grilled Crostini (see page 24)
'Zuppa di poveri' ('soup of the poor') was one of the first soups we cooked in the River Cafe when we made it with purple sprouting broccoli. This version uses wild asparagus or thin sprue. The basis of the soup is a good chicken stock – very much part of the Italian kitchen – with toasted bread and grated Parmesan which melts into the broth.

Risi Bisi Verde (see page 26)
Risi bisi is the risotto traditionally cooked in Venice when the new peas come into season. This recipe has the addition of spinach and mint which go well with peas. Looking a dramatic bright green, the recipe is a cross between a thick soup and a soupy risotto.

Cannellini Bean and Parsley Soup (see page 27)
This is a favourite Italian way of using beans. It is incredibly simple with only three basic ingredients: parsley, garlic and beans. It should be seasoned well before pouring on fine, peppery Tuscan oil.

Spicy Mussel Soup (see page 28)
This Neapolitan recipe is made with generous amounts of mussels, chillies, anchovies and tomatoes to create a dense, hot, peppery soup.

Chickpea and Porcini Soup (see page 30)

Chickpeas vary in size; use the largest ones you can find. More importantly, ask for the new season's chickpeas – the ones harvested in August and September. The skins of old chickpeas become tough, the flavour fades, and they will take almost twice as long to cook.

Acquacotta di Ricotta (see page 32)

'Acquacotta' means 'cooked water' in Italian. These soups are made with toasted bread, vegetables and water rather than stock. This version combines the flavours of potatoes, cannellini beans and ricotta with the sharp taste of bitter greens. This is a wonderful soup to enjoy with the new season's spicy green olive oil.

Summer Ribollita

500 g (18 oz) fresh borlotti or
    cannellini beans (podded
    weight)
extra virgin olive oil
4 young onions, red or white,
    peeled and chopped
1 head celery, plus leaves, stalks
    chopped
1 head fresh garlic, peeled and
    sliced
500 g (18 oz) Swiss chard stalks
    and leaves, stalks sliced into
    large matchsticks
1 bunch fresh basil, leaves picked
    from the stalks
1 bunch fresh mint, leaves picked
    from the stalks
1 bunch fresh marjoram, leaves
    picked from the stalks
1 bunch fresh flat-leaf parsley,
    leaves picked from the stalks

2 kg (4.1/2 lb) fresh ripe plum
    tomatoes, skinned, seeded and
    chopped
Maldon salt and freshly ground
    black pepper
1 bunch fresh borage (optional)
300 g (10 oz) fresh spinach,
    tough stalks removed
2 loaves ciabatta bread, stale if
    possible, crusts removed
1 fresh red chilli

For eight

Prepare the beans as described on page 134.

In a large, heavy pan heat 3 tablespoons of olive oil, then add the onion and celery stalks. Stir and cook gently until they are soft and brown. Add the garlic and chard stalks and continue to cook. When the garlic begins to colour, add half the basil, mint, marjoram, parsley and celery leaves. Gently fry and stir together to combine the herbs, then add the chopped tomatoes. Season and simmer for 30 minutes: the tomatoes should reduce with the vegetables.

Separately, in another large saucepan full of boiling water with plenty of salt, blanch the borage and chard leaves and then the spinach. Drain, keeping the blanching water, and roughly chop. Add the leaves to the vegetable and tomato mixture along with the cooked beans. Tear up the ciabatta into 3-5 cm (1-2 in) lengths and add to the soup. Pour over some of the blanching water to moisten the bread, and stir in the remaining herbs. Check for seasoning, then add salt and pepper to taste and 3 tablespoons of olive oil. The consistency should be very thick.

Remove the seeds and fibres from the inside of the red chilli by cutting it in half and scraping with a teaspoon. Chop the chilli roughly, then place in a small bowl and add 2 tablespoons of the extra virgin olive oil. Dribble this chilli sauce over each bowl before serving.

Tuscan Bread, Tomato and Basil Soup

4 garlic cloves, peeled and cut
    into slivers
175 ml (6 fl oz) olive oil
4 kg (9 lb) ripe sweet tomatoes,
    skinned and seeded, or 2 kg
    (4.1/2 lb) tinned plum
    tomatoes, drained of most of
    their juices
Maldon salt and freshly ground
    black pepper
600 ml (1 pint) cold water
4 loaves stale ciabatta or other
    sourdough bread
1 large bunch fresh basil, leaves
    picked from stalks
extra virgin olive oil

For ten

Put the garlic and the olive oil into a heavy saucepan and cook gently for a few minutes. Just before the garlic turns brown, add all the tomatoes. Simmer for 30 minutes, stirring occasionally, until the tomatoes become concentrated. Season with salt and pepper, then add the water and bring to the boil.

Cut most of the crust off the bread and pull into pieces. Put the bread into the tomato mixture and stir until the bread absorbs the liquid, adding more boiling water if it is too thick.

Remove from the heat and allow to cool slightly. If the basil leaves are large, tear into pieces. Stir into the soup with 120-175 ml (4-6 fl oz) of the extra virgin olive oil. Let the soup sit before serving to allow the bread to absorb the flavour of the basil and oil. Add more of the extra virgin olive oil to each bowl.

Chestnut, Pumpkin and Farro Soup

1 kg (2.1/4 lb) fresh chestnuts,
  boiled, peeled and roughly
  chopped, or 600 g (1.1/4 lb)
  prepeeled whole cooked
  chestnuts, rinsed thoroughly
1 kg (2.1/4 lb) roasted pumpkin
  (see page 141)
150 g (5 oz) farro, soaked in cold
  water for 1/2 hour
100 ml (3.1/2 fl oz) olive oil
1 red onion, peeled and finely
  chopped
1 head celery, roughly chopped
150 g (5 oz) pancetta, cut into
  matchsticks
2 garlic cloves, peeled and
  chopped
50 g (2 oz) fresh rosemary,
  chopped
2 dried red chillies, crumbled
1 litre (1.3/4 pints) Chicken Broth
  (see page 22), warmed
Maldon salt and freshly ground
  black pepper
extra virgin olive oil
50 g (2 oz) Parmesan

For six

Drain the farro, then put in a pan, cover with cold water, and bring to the boil. Cook until the farro expands and is al dente, about 20 minutes.

Roughly chop the roasted pumpkin. Meanwhile, in a heavy saucepan large enough to hold the soup, heat 3 tablespoons of the olive oil.

Add the onion and celery, fry gently to soften, then add the pancetta, garlic, chopped rosemary and chillies. Allow this to cook on a low heat until the pancetta and garlic begin to colour, then add the chestnuts. Let them absorb the pancetta flavours, about 5 minutes, then add the pumpkin. Cook this for a further 5 minutes, then add the warmed chicken broth. Finally add the cooked farro.

Heat through, check for seasoning, then serve with grated Parmesan and drizzled with extra virgin olive oil.

Chicken Broth

1 x 1.5-2 kg (3.1/4-4.1/2 lb)
    mature, organic, free-range
    boiling hen or large chicken,
    all fatty parts removed
1 small red onion, peeled
2 large carrots, scrubbed
1 head celery, white parts only,
    washed
2 tomatoes
1 head garlic, unpeeled
1 bunch parsley stalks
3 sprigs fresh thyme
5 bay leaves
1 teaspoon black peppercorns
3 litres (5 pints) cold water
Maldon salt

Makes 2 litres (3.1/2 pints)

Put the chicken and the rest of the ingredients, apart from the salt, into a large saucepan, and bring gently to the boil. Turn the heat down and skim, then gently simmer for about 1 hour. Remove the chicken and strain out the vegetables and herbs. Season the broth.

Fish Broth

Bones and trimmings of 1 turbot
    including the head, halibut or
    monkfish
2 red onions, peeled and cut in
    quarters lengthways
2 carrots, sliced
4 celery stalks
1 fennel bulb, untrimmed, cut in
    half
1/2 head garlic, peeled
a few fresh flat-leaf parsley stalks
2 bay leaves
1 tablespoon fennel seeds
6 white or black peppercorns
2 dried red chillies
2 litres (3.1/2 pints) cold water
150 ml (5 fl oz) white wine
    (optional)
Maldon salt and freshly ground
    black pepper

Makes 2 litres (3.1/2 pints)

Put the fish bones, head and trimmings into a large saucepan, add the vegetables, herbs and spices, cover with the cold water and add the wine if using. Bring to the boil, skimming off the scum as it comes to the surface. Lower the heat and simmer gently for 15-20 minutes; in order to achieve a fresh-tasting stock, do not be tempted to do so for longer than this. Season generously, strain and use immediately.

Asparagus Broth with Grilled Crostini

1.5 kg (3.1/4 lb) thin asparagus,
   or sprue
2 litres (3.1/2 pints) Chicken
   Broth, strained (see page 22)
Maldon salt and freshly ground
   black pepper
6 slices ciabatta, cut on the
   diagonal
2 garlic cloves, peeled
100-150 g (4-5 oz) Parmesan,
   freshly grated

For six

Wash and prepare the asparagus by snapping off and keeping only the most tender parts of the stems. Slice the stems and tips quite thinly on a diagonal.

Bring the broth to the boil and leave to simmer. Check it for seasoning and then add the asparagus. While they are cooking, about 1-2 minutes, grill the ciabatta on both sides. Rub with garlic and place each slice in the middle of a warm soup plate.

Sprinkle some of the Parmesan over the crostini. Ladle the asparagus and broth over the top of the crostini so that the broth soaks into it and melts the cheese.

Serve with the remaining Parmesan sprinkled over the asparagus.

Risi Bisi Verde

2 litres (3.1/2 pints) Chicken Broth
(see page 22)
Maldon salt and freshly ground
black pepper
1 kg (2.1/4 lb) fresh young peas
(podded weight)
1 kg (2.1/4 lb) washed spinach
leaves, tough stems removed
1 bunch fresh mint, tough stalks
removed
60 g (2.1/2 oz) unsalted butter
1/2 large red onion, peeled and
finely chopped
1/2 head celery, cleaned and
finely chopped
100 g (4 oz) pancetta affumicata
or smoked streaky bacon,
finely chopped
1 garlic clove, peeled and finely
chopped
300 g (10 oz) carnaroli rice

For six

Heat the chicken broth to a simmer and check for seasoning.

Bring a large saucepan of water to the boil with a good pinch of sea salt, and into this put the peas, spinach and mint. Allow to cook for just a minute or so, until the peas are half cooked, then remove from the water and place half the vegetables in the blender. Pulse-chop in short bursts with a ladle of hot broth. It should be pulsed until quite rough, not to a purée. The remaining vegetables need to be roughly chopped by hand to keep their texture.

In a large, heavy-bottomed pan, heat the butter, add the onion and celery and stir together until they soften and become translucent. Add the pancetta and stir until it begins to soften, then add the garlic and continue to cook on a low heat.

Add the rice and stir to coat with the butter until it starts to become transparent. Start to add the hot broth ladle by ladle, allowing each ladleful to be absorbed before you add the next. Stir constantly until the rice is cooked. Add a couple more ladles of broth, as you want a soupy consistency.

Stir in the pulsed vegetables and the roughly chopped vegetables. They need to be brought up to the temperature of the rice before serving.

Cannellini Bean and Parsley Soup

For the beans

250 g (9 oz) dried cannellini
beans

4 tablespoons bicarbonate of
soda

2 large fresh tomatoes

a handful fresh sage leaves

1 bulb garlic, unpeeled

2-3 garlic cloves, peeled and
chopped

3 tablespoons olive oil

1 bunch fresh flat-leaf parsley,
leaves chopped

Maldon salt and freshly ground
black pepper

extra virgin olive oil

For six

To prepare the dried beans first soak them overnight in a bowl of cold water to which you have added the bicarbonate of soda. Drain and rinse the beans well, then place in a saucepan, cover with fresh cold water and bring to the boil. Simmer for 10 minutes, then drain again. Pour in enough fresh water to cover by about 5cm (2 in), then add the tomatoes, sage and garlic. Return to the boil and simmer, covered, occasionally removing any scum that comes to the surface, until tender, which can vary from 40-90 minutes. When the beans are tender, remove the tomato, sage and garlic but keep the beans in the cooking water until ready to use.

Drain the beans and reserve the liquid. In a large saucepan, cook the garlic in the oil until soft but not brown. Add the parsley and cook for a second, then add the beans and stir.

Put three-quarters of the mixture into a food processor with some of the liquid, and briefly pulse; you do not want a purée. Add more liquid if necessary, but it should be thick. Return to the saucepan and season with salt and pepper. If too thick, add more cooking liquid. Serve with a generous amount of extra virgin olive oil.

Spicy Mussel Soup

2.5 kg (5.1/2 lb) mussels, cleaned
75 ml (2.1/2 fl oz) olive oil
150 ml (5 fl oz) white wine
120 ml (4 fl oz) cold water
4 garlic cloves, peeled and finely
   chopped
6 anchovy fillets
3 small dried chillies, crumbled
1 x 800 g (1.3/4 lb) tin peeled
   plum tomatoes, drained of
   most of their juices, chopped
Maldon salt and freshly ground
   black pepper
1 bunch fresh flat-leaf parsley,
   chopped

For six

Clean the mussels very thoroughly under cold running water. Scrub well with a stiff brush, and scrape off any barnacles. Discard any that are open or have cracked or broken shells.

Heat 60 ml (2 fl oz) of the olive oil in a saucepan, then add the mussels, the white wine and the water. Cook over a high heat until all the mussels are open, discarding any that remain closed. You may need to cook the mussels in batches; divide the oil, wine and water accordingly.

Remove the mussels, and boil to reduce the liquid by half. Remove the mussels from their shells.

Heat the remaining olive oil in a large pan and fry the garlic until lightly brown. Add the anchovies, and mash with the garlic into the hot oil until dissolved. Add the mussel liquid, chillies and tomatoes. Cook gently until the tomatoes have reduced to a medium-thick consistency. This should take about 30 minutes. Season with salt and pepper and more chilli if necessary. Finally, put in the mussels and the remaining parsley.

Chickpea and Porcini Soup

50 g (2 oz) dried porcini,
    reconstituted, plus their liquid
    strained of any grit
150 g (5 oz) dried chickpeas,
    soaked overnight in water or
    2 x 225 g (8 oz) tins
    chickpeas, drained and rinsed
1 large potato, peeled
1/2 head garlic
1/4 head celery
Maldon salt and freshly ground
    black pepper
extra virgin olive oil
1 small red onion, peeled and
    chopped
1/2 head celery, white parts
    removed
1 small bunch fresh flat-leaf
    parsley, stalks removed
2 garlic cloves, peeled and finely
    chopped
4 anchovy fillets
1 kg (2.1/4 lb) Swiss chard, leaves
    and stalks

To serve
6 slices ciabatta, cut at an angle
1 garlic clove, peeled and halved
160 g (5.1/2 oz) Parmesan, freshly
    grated

For six

Pat the porcini dry. Put the chickpeas into a saucepan with the potato, 1/4 head celery and 1/2 head garlic. Cover with water and bring to the boil and skim the surface. Turn down the heat and simmer for 1-1.1/2 hours. Drain half the cooking liquid from the chickpeas and season with salt and pepper.

Using a large, thick-bottomed saucepan, heat 2 tablespoons of the olive oil and gently fry the onion with the celery until they begin to colour. Add the parsley, garlic and anchovies and cook together for 5 minutes to blend the flavours.

Cut the white part of the chard stalks into 1 cm (1/2 in) slices and add to the soup base. Roughly chop the soaked porcini pieces and add this as well. Stir and fry together for 3-4 minutes. Add half of the cooked chickpeas and a ladleful of their cooking liquid or water. Bring to the boil, then turn down the heat and simmer for 15 minutes. Mash the remaining chickpeas and add to the soup. Stir well and check for seasoning. Separately blanch the green part of the chard. Drain, roughly chop and then add to the soup.

Toast the ciabatta, and rub each slice with garlic. Divide among your soup bowls. Ladle over the soup, sprinkle with Parmesan and drizzle with extra virgin olive oil.

Acquacotta di Ricotta

350 g (12 oz) fresh ricotta
2 tablespoons olive oil
1 red onion, peeled and chopped
1/2 head celery, including leaves,
  chopped
2 garlic cloves, chopped
1 small bunch fresh flat-leaf
  parsley, chopped
2 small dried red chillies
4 medium potatoes (yellow, waxy
  variety), peeled
225 g (8 oz) dried cannellini
  beans, soaked and cooked
  (see page 27) or 1 x 225 g
  (8 oz) tin cannellini beans,
  drained and rinsed
500 g (18 oz) bitter greens
  (cicoria or spinach and
  dandelion)
Maldon salt and freshly ground
  black pepper

To serve
6 slices sourdough bread
1 garlic clove, peeled
extra virgin olive oil
70 g (3 oz) Parmesan

For six

Soak and cook the beans as described on page 27. Drain.

Using a large, thick-bottomed saucepan, heat the olive oil, add the onion and celery stalks and fry gently until soft and beginning to colour. Add the garlic, parsley, celery leaves and crumbled chillies. Continue to cook, stirring to combine the flavours for 3-4 minutes.

Cut the potatoes into 2 cm (3/4 in) cubes. Add the potatoes and the cannellini beans to the saucepan, stir and just cover with hot water. Cover and gently simmer for 15-20 minutes, or until the potatoes are al dente.

Blanch the cicoria or spinach and dandelion for 2 minutes. Drain, cool and roughly chop. The greens should remain quite tough.

Add the greens, stir, and continue to cook for 3 or 4 minutes. Season with salt and pepper. Break up the ricotta with a fork and stir into the soup.

To serve, grill the sourdough on both sides and rub one side only with garlic. Tear the bruschetta in half and place the pieces in warm soup bowls. Ladle over the soup. Crumble over the rest of the ricotta, drizzle with extra virgin olive oil and serve with grated Parmesan.

Pasta, Risotto and Polenta

Penne, spaghetti, conchiglie, tagliatelle, pappardelle, farfalle and rigatoni – each of these types of pasta is cooked with very specific types of sauce. They range from the exquisitely simple Spaghetti with Lemon to the more rich and complex Pappardelle with Hare.

In the spring series the pastas were light, using fresh tomatoes, rocket, lemon and peas. In the autumn series we celebrate the arrival of the precious white truffle, using it on its own with tagliatelle, and the simple dark cabbage, cavolo nero, with the new olive oil and and penne.

Risotto, regional to the Veneto, is best made at home for a small number of people. We show you the basic method for making risotto because, once you have learnt this, all you need for a perfect risotto is the right rice, good stock and the time, care and concentration while you cook.

The choice of rice for a particular risotto is important. Arborio rice is the most widely available risotto rice as there is more production of this type than any other. It is a long grain rice which absorbs flavours easily, and the period during which it remains al dente is longer than that of other varieties. Carnaroli rice is not produced in the same quantities as arborio and is consequently more expensive. Like arborio it has a long grain but it is less polished which makes it a little more difficult to cook and get right. It is delicious, though, and we feel that the extra care is worth it. Vialone nano rice is rounder and each grain can absorb twice its weight in liquid. It is chosen by the Venetians for their very wet, soupy risotto nero or risi e bisi.

Polenta is one of the staples of the northernmost regions in Italy. Most people don't realise that it is also very seasonal. The corn is grown in the summer, then harvested in October, after which it is dried and milled. Bramata polenta is the traditional blend made from five different varieties of corn – some with small, even yellow kernels, some with larger orange ones, some with a mixture of kernels on the same cob. The wheat germ is removed so that only the outside of the kernel is ground. It is the blending which gives the finished Bramata so much flavour and it is the one we always choose to use.

Spaghetti with Lemon (see page 46)

This is probably one of the most successful pasta recipes in our books. It is Genovese in origin, and very easy to make. You need only lemons, olive oil, Parmesan and a packet of spaghetti, but each of these must be of the highest quality: the best, most flavourful extra virgin olive oil; unwaxed organic lemons with lots of juice and good thick skins; top-quality dried spaghetti, and freshly grated Parmesan. The trick is to get the right amount of lemon juice, but this is difficult to specify in a recipe as lemons vary so much in size and juiciness. Use your sense and taste when you stir in the olive oil and Parmesan: if it's too lemony, add more oil and cheese.

Rigatoni with Pecorino, Tomato, Butter and Balsamic Vinegar (see page 47)

This is a combination of ingredients from the north (the balsamic and butter) with Pecorino and tomatoes from the south. The generous amount of butter is melted on to the pasta, and should coat each tube. Then the balsamic vinegar is added to flavour and colour the pasta; the tomato sauce is gently folded through the pasta, not totally mixed in. Lastly, grated Pecorino, a softer, saltier cheese than Parmesan, is stirred through. This sweet pasta is very popular with children. Large penne rigate works just as well as rigatoni in this recipe.

Conchiglie with Ricotta and Rocket (see page 48)

This pasta sauce is very simple and quick to cook. The shape of conchiglie is perfect for holding a sauce of this consistency. The ricotta is mild so it is combined with the strong flavours of the rocket and chilli. Try to find ricotta in basket-impressed mounds; this will be fresh, crumbly and moist.

Rocket leaves vary; we grow the large-leaved rocket, the thinner, spear-like Capri rocket and the wild, very peppery Turkish variety. Try to buy bunches of mature rocket from ethnic shops or markets, large leaved, and dark green in colour, as they have more flavour.

In this recipe, half the rocket is cooked until it wilts, when the flavour is subtle; the remainder is added at the end, so the rocket retains its pepperiness and texture.

Farfalle with Mint, Prosciutto and Peas (see page 50)

Farfalle, known as butterfly or bow-tie pasta, can take a thick sauce. This pea sauce uses the lovely young peas that arrive in the early summer, though it can be made with frozen petit pois. If some of the pods are larger than others it is really worth grading the peas as you shell them. The larger peas take longer to cook so add the small, sweet ones at the end.

Ziti Carbonara with Salami and Sage (see page 52)

Ziti is a long, fat tube-shaped pasta. When cooked they are difficult to pile on the plate but delicious nevertheless as the egg sauce runs down both the inside and the outside of the tubes.

Carbonara is usually made with pancetta. In this recipe we use a coarse spicy, peppery salami called Felino. Buy it in the piece with its skin on, and ask for a soft one.

Spaghetti with Crab (see page 53)

If possible, buy live crabs and cook them yourself for this sauce. There are two reasons for this. One, you can make sure that you don't overcook the crabs which makes the meat harder and less flavourful, and two, warm crabmeat is still slightly soft so it comes out of the shell more easily. If you buy a crab that is already cooked, the meat will be cold so it becomes more difficult to mix with the other ingredients.

We buy male crabs as they have more white meat and use the long, red Dutch chillies which are not too hot, an addition which is probably more River Cafe than traditional.

Tagliatelle with White Truffles (see page 54)

This is a dish for a very special occasion, as truffles are expensive. It is a very seasonal treat, for the white truffles from Alba in Piedmont are only available from October to January. Truffles are unique among vegetables as their pungent aroma overwhelms you even more than their taste. The price can vary enormously, as can the quality; they should feel firm. People often store them in rice or among eggs, both of which absorb the truffle flavour, but if you are going to use the truffle for shaving over pasta or risotto, wrap it in very light kitchen or tissue paper which has been moistened and then put in a sealed box in the lower part of the fridge.

The 'sauce' is simply a little of the pasta cooking water, some butter, Parmesan, and then lots of white truffle shaved over the top. Preferably use a truffle shaver, or alternatively a very fine potato shaver. Fine shavings are vital because as you shave you break the tiny little cells which contain the flavour molecules (thick shavings would release much less).

Pappardelle with Hare (see page 56)

Pappardelle is a fresh pasta ribbon, up to 2.5 cm (1 in) wide. Adding fine polenta flour to the white flour gives texture to the pasta. You can buy handmade Italian pappardelle dried. The thicker the pasta the sturdier it is, and will hold its shape when tossed with the rich, thick gamey sauce, the only fresh meat sauce we make at the River Cafe.

This sauce is made with hare meat that has been marinated over several days in Chianti Classico, and then cooked slowly in its marinade.

Penne with Cavolo Nero and New Olive Oil (see page 58)

Cavolo nero is one of the cabbages that should only be cooked having been exposed to frost, when the texture and flavour are fantastic. Once again, this recipe is made only when the basic ingredients are available at the same time. In November, when cavolo nero is found in every Tuscan vegetable garden, the frosts have started and so have the oil presses producing thick, peppery green oil.

Risotto with Borlotti Beans (see page 59)

The idea of having borlotti beans with rice may appear unusual, two carbohydrates together, but this is a tradition. The flavour of the risotto comes from adding pancetta and rosemary to the base. The borlotti beans are cooked separately. A small amount of the beans is then puréed, and stirred through the risotto to make it more creamy before adding the whole beans.

Black Risotto (see page 60)

The 'black' of the recipe title comes from the ink of octopus and cuttlefish. The ink is found in a sac inside the body. In octopuses it is the size of gull's eggs, in cuttlefish it is much smaller and sweeter. The sac is hard and silvery: take care when bursting it as the ink stains. The ink is thick and sometimes grainy with a wonderful sweet smell, not at all fishy. Pound it in a pestle and mortar until it is the consistency of double cream. The bodies and tentacles of the cuttlefish are cut up and fried separately as the Venetians do.

Never serve Parmesan cheese with fish risotto. Instead, use extra virgin olive oil to drizzle over at the end.

Risotto with Clams and Zucchini (see page 62)

The clams usually eaten with spaghetti in Italy are small

and sweet, and are fished all around the coast, particularly in the early summer. Do not overcook them, and be sure to keep the fragrant juices. The fennel, anchovy and Martini all contribute flavour to the risotto; the zucchini add freshness and colour.

Wet Polenta with Fresh Porcini (see page 63)

In the autumn, when the new season's polenta has just arrived, serve it with the fresh porcini which are available. You can use the softer large mushrooms with open caps as well as the young firm ones. Use the stalks as they are equally delicious.

Grilled Polenta with Slow-Cooked Tomato Sauce (see page 64)

This sauce was taught to us by an Italian, and it has an incredibly intense flavour. It is cooked for a long time, in order to let all the liquid juices evaporate. You are left with a very thick sauce to which you can add basil at the last minute; in the winter you could substitute marjoram.

Grilled Polenta with Mascarpone, Marjoram and Gorgonzola (see page 65)

This sauce consists purely of mascarpone melted with Gorgonzola. The mascarpone is very creamy in contrast to the sharpness of the Gorgonzola, and both are perfectly complemented by fresh marjoram, the one herb able to cut through that creaminess.

Spaghetti with Lemon

500 g (1 lb 2 oz) spaghetti (or spaghettini)
Maldon salt and freshly ground black pepper
juice and finely grated zest of 3-4 organic lemons, the freshest possible
150 ml (5 fl oz) olive oil
150 g (5 oz) Parmesan, freshly grated
2 handfuls fresh basil, leaves finely chopped

For six

Cook the spaghetti in a generous amount of boiling salted water, then drain thoroughly and return to the saucepan.

Meanwhile, beat the lemon juice with the olive oil, then stir in the Parmesan until thick and creamy. The Parmesan will melt into the mixture. Season, and add more lemon juice to taste.

Add the sauce to the spaghetti, and shake the pan so that each strand is coated with the cheese. Finally, stir in the chopped basil and some of the grated lemon zest.

Rigatoni with Pecorino, Tomato, Butter and Balsamic Vinegar

2 tablespoons olive oil

2 garlic cloves, peeled and cut into slivers

a handful fresh basil

1 x 800 g (1.3/4 lb) tin peeled plum tomatoes

Maldon salt and freshly ground black pepper

500 g (1 lb 2 oz) rigatoni

75 g (3 oz) butter, cut into pieces

4 tablespoons balsamic vinegar, 10-year-old plus

120 g (4.1/2 oz) Pecorino cheese, freshly grated

For six

Heat the oil in a large pan and gently fry the garlic until light brown. Add a few of the basil leaves and then the tomatoes. Stir and cook gently for 30-40 minutes, until reduced to a thick sauce. Season with salt and pepper and add the remaining basil.

Cook the pasta in a generous amount of boiling salted water, drain thoroughly and return to the saucepan with the butter. When this has melted, add the balsamic vinegar and toss over a gentle heat for a few seconds until the pasta tubes are brown in colour. Throw in a handful of the grated Pecorino, and finally gently fold in the tomato sauce. Serve with more Pecorino.

Conchiglie with Ricotta and Rocket

1 kg (2.1/4 lb) rocket leaves

100 ml (3.1/2 fl oz) extra virgin
olive oil

3 garlic cloves, peeled and
roughly chopped

4 tablespoons fresh basil leaves,
torn into pieces

2 fresh red chillies, seeded and
chopped

Maldon salt and fresh ground
black pepper

400 g (14 oz) conchiglie

200 g (7 oz) ricotta, lightly
beaten with a fork

150 g (5 oz) Parmesan, freshly
grated

For six

Wash the rocket and dry in a salad spinner. Divide the quantity into two, and roughly chop one half.

Heat a large, thick-bottomed saucepan and add 2 tablespoons of the oil. Gently fry the garlic until it begins to turn gold, then add the torn-up basil leaves and the whole rocket leaves. Put on the lid and let the rocket wilt – this takes 2-3 minutes. Put the hot wilted rocket and any liquid in the pan into a food processor and pulse-chop. Add half of the chopped rocket and blend again to combine. Stir in the chilli, salt, pepper and the remaining olive oil.

Cook the pasta in a generous amount of boiling salted water. Drain, return to the pan, and add the rocket sauce. Turn the pasta over gently to coat each shell. Finally, lightly fork in the ricotta and the remaining chopped rocket. Season, and serve with the Parmesan.

Farfalle with Mint, Prosciutto and Peas

2 kg (4.1/2 lb) young fresh peas
in their pods or 150 g (5 oz)
frozen petits pois
50 g (2 oz) unsalted butter
1 medium red onion or sweet
white onion, peeled and
chopped
1 bunch fresh mint, stalks
removed, roughly chopped
10 slices prosciutto di Parma
150 ml (5 fl oz) double cream
Maldon salt and freshly ground
black pepper
500 g (18 oz) farfalle
100 g (4 oz) Parmesan, freshly
grated

For six

Using a thick-bottomed saucepan, gently heat the butter. Add the onion and fry gently until soft and beginning to colour. Add the peas and one-third of the mint and stir to combine. Pour over enough water to just cover the peas, then carefully place 4 slices of prosciutto on the top. Simmer very gently for 5-10 minutes, or until the peas are soft, adding more water if the level goes below that of the peas.

Put half the sauce into a blender, including the prosciutto. Add half of the remaining mint and pulse-chop to a rough texture. Return to the pan and stir to combine the two different textured sauces. Add the cream, the remaining mint, salt and pepper and bring to the boil. Remove from the heat and add the remaining peas.

Cook the farfalle in a generous amount of boiling salted water, drain and add to the sauce.

Tear the remaining prosciutto into smaller pieces and add to the pasta mixture. Serve with the Parmesan.

Ziti Carbonara with Salami and Sage

500 g (1 lb 2 oz) ziti (or other
    long, thick, tube pasta)
Maldon salt and coarsely ground
    black pepper
1 tablespoon unsalted butter
2 tablespoons olive oil
1 x 500 g (18 oz) piece of Felino
    salami, peeled and cut into
    thick matchsticks
1 small dried red chilli
12 sage leaves, stalks removed
75 ml (2.1/2 fl oz) white wine
8 organic egg yolks
100 ml (3.1/2 fl oz) double cream
75 g (3 oz) Parmesan, freshly
    grated

For six

Cook the ziti in a generous amount of boiling salted water. This will take 12 minutes.

Meanwhile, heat the butter and oil together in a frying pan and when hot, add the salami pieces and allow to brown on all sides. Add the chilli and then the sage leaves and continue to fry, stirring together to allow the flavours to combine. Finally add the wine and allow to reduce for 30 seconds.

Beat the egg yolks lightly with a fork and season generously with salt and pepper. Add the cream and half the Parmesan.

Check the pasta, drain and return to the saucepan. Add the hot salami and sage mixture together with all the juices from the pan. Stir together and then pour in the egg mixture. The sauce will immediately thicken. Serve on to warm individual plates, scattered with the remaining Parmesan.

Spaghetti with Crab

2 live crabs, approximately
  1-1.6 kg (2.1/2-3.1/2 lb) each in
  weight
3 fresh red chillies, seeded and
  finely chopped
3 handfuls fresh flat-leaf parsley,
  finely chopped
juice of 4 lemons
3 garlic cloves, peeled and
  ground to a paste with a little
  salt
250 ml (8 fl oz) olive oil
500 g (18 oz) spaghetti
Maldon salt and freshly ground
  black pepper
extra virgin olive oil

For six

Place each crab in a large saucepan, cover with cold water, replace the lid and slowly bring to the boil. This will take up to 30 minutes. Boil for 4 minutes, remove the crabs from the water and cool.

First remove the claws and legs. Break the bodies open carefully. Remove the brown meat from inside the shell and transfer along with any juices to a bowl. Remove the white meat from the claws and legs and add to the brown meat in the bowl. Finally pick out the whitemeat from the bodies. Mix together.

Add the chillies and most of the chopped parsley, the lemon juice and crushed garlic to the crab mixture. Stir in the olive oil. This sauce should be quite liquid.

Cook the pasta in a generous amount of boiling salted water then drain thoroughly. Stir into the crab sauce, but do not reheat. Serve sprinkled with the remaining chopped parsley and a generous amount of extra virgin olive oil.

Tagliatelle with White Truffles

30 g (1.1/4 oz) white truffles per person
600 g (1 lb 6 oz) fresh tagliatelle (or tagliarini) or 450 g (1 lb) dried egg tagliatelle (or tagliarini)
Maldon salt and freshly ground black pepper
200 g (7 oz) unsalted butter, softened
3 tablespoons freshly grated Parmesan

For four

Clean the truffles with a soft brush to remove all sand and grit. If there is any clay clinging, use a damp cloth or small pointed knife to scrape it off. Never wash truffles.

Cook the pasta in a generous amount of boiling salted water, then drain thoroughly, saving a little of the water. Stir in three-quarters of the softened butter and a few tablespoons of the pasta water. Season with salt and pepper, add the Parmesan, and toss together.

Grate the first few shavings from each truffle into the pasta, and toss. Serve on warm plates, and place a little knob of the remaining softened butter on top. Generously shave the truffles all over each portion. Serve with extra Parmesan.

Pappardelle with Hare

For the marinade
1 bottle Chianti Classico
1 head garlic, cut into 4 pieces
1 red onion, quartered
1/2 head celery, cut into 3
6 bay leaves
10 juniper berries
2 cinnamon sticks
2 tablespoons peppercorns

1 small hare, jointed into small
    pieces (legs and saddle
    divided into 4 pieces)
4 tablespoons olive oil
flour for dusting
Maldon salt and freshly ground
    black pepper
1 large onion, finely chopped
1 carrot, finely chopped
3 celery stalks, finely chopped
2 garlic cloves, finely chopped
3 cloves
6 juniper berries
1 cinnamon stick
250 g (9 oz) fresh pappardelle
3 tablespoons double cream
2 tablespoons Parmesan

For six

Place the pieces of hare in a dish large enough to contain all the ingredients of the marinade. Make sure the hare is covered by the wine. Turn over the hare after 24 hours. Leave to marinade for a total of 3 days. Remove the hare from the marinade and pat dry. Strain the liquid and discard the vegetables and spices.

Heat half the olive oil in a heavy-bottomed pan. Dust the hare pieces in flour seasoned with salt and pepper, and then fry in the hot oil until evenly browned and well coloured. Remove from the pan and set aside. Pour the remaining oil into the pan, lower the heat, and soften the onion, carrot and celery until they start to caramelise, about 15 minutes.

Add the garlic and cook for a further 15 minutes. Pour in enough marinade to just cover the hare and allow to reduce for a further 10 minutes. Lower the heat to a gentle simmer and add the cloves, juniper, cinnamon, salt and pepper and the hare pieces. Cook gently for 1 hour, turning the pieces over from time to time. Add more of the marinade if the liquid in the pan becomes too thick.

After an hour the saddle pieces will be cooked, so remove and put to one side, leaving the legs to cook for a further 30-50 minutes. If the sauce seems dry, add a little boiling water, about 120 ml (4 fl oz). Remove the meat from both the saddle and legs, keeping the two meats separate, and then break into pieces.

Discard the cloves and cinnamon from the sauce. Put the sauce and leg meat through a food mill or into a liquidiser, and pulse until all the meat has been finely chopped. Put in a saucepan with the cream and saddle meat, heat through and check for seasoning.

Cook the pappardelle. Drain thoroughly, combine with the sauce, and serve immediately with the freshly grated Parmesan.

Penne with Cavolo Nero and New Olive Oil

2 kg (4 lb 8 oz) cavolo nero
 leaves
Maldon salt and freshly ground
 black pepper
4 garlic cloves, peeled
250 ml (8 fl oz) extra virgin olive
 oil
500 g (1 lb 2 oz) penne
Parmesan, freshly grated

For six

Remove the tough stalks of the cavolo nero leaves. Keeping the leaves as whole as possible, blanch them in a generous amount of boiling salted water with 2 garlic cloves for 5 minutes only. Drain well. Put the blanched garlic and cavolo nero in the food processor and pulse-chop to a coarse purée. In the last couple of pulses, pour 75 ml (2.1/2 fl oz) of the extra virgin olive oil into the processor. This makes a dark green liquid purée.

Crush the 2 remaining garlic cloves with 1 teaspoon salt. Stir into the purée along with a further 75 ml (2.1/2 fl oz) oil. Season to taste.

Cook the penne in a generous amount of boiling salted water, then drain thoroughly. Put the pasta into the sauce and stir until each piece is thickly coated. Pour in the remaining olive oil and serve with the Parmesan.

Risotto with Borlotti Beans

400 g (14 oz) dried borlotti
  beans, soaked and cooked
  (see page 27)
1 litre (1.3/4 pints) Chicken Broth
  (see page 22)
Maldon salt and freshly ground
  black pepper
80 g (3.1/4 oz) unsalted butter
2-3 tablespoons olive oil
1 head celery, white tender parts
  only, roughly chopped
1 small red onion, peeled and
  finely chopped
100 g (4 oz) pancetta affumicata,
  cut into matchsticks
3 garlic cloves, peeled and finely
  chopped
1 small bunch fresh rosemary,
  stalks removed and leaves very
  finely chopped
400 g (14 oz) carnaroli rice
200 g (7 oz) Parmesan, freshly
  grated

For six

Drain the soaked, cooked beans.

Heat the chicken broth to a simmer, and check for seasoning.

In a heavy-bottomed saucepan, heat the butter and olive oil. Add the celery and onion and cook on a low heat for a few minutes. Add the pancetta, then when it becomes soft and slightly coloured, add the chopped garlic and rosemary. Before the garlic begins to colour, add the rice, stirring until it is coated with the oil and butter, about 5 minutes.

Start adding the hot broth, ladle by ladle. Allow each ladleful of broth to be absorbed by the rice before adding the next, stirring all the time. Towards the end of cooking, about 20 minutes, purée half the borlotti beans, add to the rice and stir them in. The rice should have a creamy consistency but should remain al dente. Add the remaining whole beans, the butter and about half the grated Parmesan.

Serve with more grated Parmesan and a knob of butter.

Black Risotto

1 kg (2.1/4 lb) small cuttlefish
2 tablespoons olive oil
4 garlic cloves, peeled and finely chopped
2 small dried chillies
juice of 2 lemons
Maldon salt and freshly ground black pepper
1 litre (1.3/4 pints) Fish Broth (see page 23)
75 g (3 oz) butter
400 g (14 oz) vialone nano rice
120 ml (4 fl oz) white wine, like Pinot Grigio
3 sachets squid or cuttlefish ink
2 tablespoons finely chopped fresh flat-leaf parsley

For six

Clean the cuttlefish by removing the blade-shaped bone and innards, reserving the ink sacs. Cut the tentacle clusters from the heads and discard the beak and any hard matter. Cut the body sacs lengthwise into strips.

Crush the ink sacs into a smooth paste in a pestle and mortar.

Using a large frying pan, heat the olive oil and add half the chopped garlic. The moment the garlic begins to colour add the cuttlefish, dried chillies and lemon juice, and season with salt and pepper. Put aside.

Heat the fish broth and check for seasoning.

Melt the butter in a thick-bottomed saucepan and fry the remaining garlic for 1 minute. Add the rice and continue to cook gently, stirring, until the rice is coated. Pour in the white wine and cook until it has been absorbed by the rice. Add a ladle of hot fish broth, stirring continually until it too has been absorbed. Continue to add more fish broth until the rice is al dente, then add the squid ink. When there is only one ladle of broth left, turn off the heat and add this remaining broth. Add the cuttlefish pieces, stir to combine totally with the risotto and scatter with the parsley.

Risotto with Clams and Zucchini

3 kg (6.1/2 lb) small clams (vongole), thoroughly washed and checked
4 tablespoons olive oil
3 garlic cloves, peeled and finely chopped
2 dried red chillies, crumbled
75 ml (2.1/2 fl oz) white wine
500 g (18 oz) zucchini, cut lengthways into four and then across into thin segments
Maldon salt and freshly ground black pepper
1.5 litres (2.1/2 pints) Fish Broth (see page 23)
1 small red onion, peeled and chopped
2 small fennel bulbs, trimmed and chopped
6 anchovy fillets
400 g (14 oz) vialone nano rice
75 ml (2.1/2 fl oz) dry Martini
juice of 2 lemons
a handful fresh flat-leaf parsley
extra virgin olive oil

For six

To open the clams, heat 2 tablespoons of the olive oil in a large saucepan and add 1 teaspoon chopped garlic and one of the chillies. When the garlic begins to colour, add the clams and the white wine. Cover with a lid, shake for a few seconds and cook for 3 minutes or until the clams have steamed open. Strain, keeping the juices, and allow to cool. When they are cool enough to touch, remove the clams from their shells and then return them to their juices and put aside.

Blanch the zucchini in salted water. Drain and keep.

Heat the fish broth and check for seasoning.

Heat the remaining olive oil in a heavy-bottomed saucepan. Add the onion and fennel and fry together, stirring over a low heat until soft and beginning to colour. Add the remaining garlic, chillies and the anchovies. Stir to combine the flavours, and break up the anchovies.

Add the rice and stir to coat each grain. Add the Martini, and stir constantly as the wine is absorbed, then reduce the heat and start adding the hot broth ladle by ladle, allowing each ladleful to be absorbed before adding the next. Continue until the rice is al dente, usually about 20 minutes. Finally stir in the clams and their juices, the lemon, zucchini and parsley. Serve with extra virgin olive oil poured over.

Wet Polenta with Fresh Porcini

For the polenta

350 g (12 oz) bramata polenta

1.75-2 litres (3-3.1/2 pints) water

Maldon salt and coarsely ground
    black pepper

150 g (5 oz) unsalted butter

200 g (7 oz) Parmesan, freshly
    grated

1 kg (2.1/4 lb) fresh porcini or
    other strong-flavoured
    mushrooms

2 tablespoons extra virgin olive
    oil

50 g (2 oz) unsalted butter

2 garlic cloves, peeled and
    chopped

2 tablespoons fresh thyme
    leaves, roughly chopped

3 tablespoons fresh flat-leaf
    parsley, stalks removed and
    leaves chopped

juice of 1 large lemon

For six

Put the polenta flour in a large jug. Bring the water to the boil in a large saucepan and add 1 teaspoon salt. Lower the heat to a simmer and slowly add the polenta flour, stirring with a whisk until completely blended. It will now start to bubble volcanically. Reduce the heat to as low as possible, and cook the polenta, stirring from time to time to prevent a skin forming on top, for about 40-45 minutes. The polenta is cooked when it falls away from the sides of the pan and has become very dense. Stir in the butter and Parmesan and season generously. Keep on a very low heat and place a piece of greaseproof paper over the surface to prevent a skin forming.

Carefully clean the mushrooms – wipe away any mud with a damp cloth and cut off any soft or maggoty bits. Roughly slice the mushrooms lengthways.

In a large, thick-bottomed saucepan, gently heat the oil and butter over a medium heat. When it is hot add the porcini, and push the slices around the pan until they begin to colour. Then add the garlic and thyme, and cook until the porcini are soft and the white parts have browned – this will take up to 10-15 minutes. Finally add the parsley, lemon juice, salt and pepper..

To serve, place the wet polenta on each plate, spoon over the porcini and some of the juices from the pan. Serve with extra Parmesan.

Grilled Polenta with Slow-Cooked Tomato Sauce

For the polenta
350 g (12 oz) bramata polenta
1.75-2 litres (3-3.1/2 pints) water
Maldon salt and freshly ground
    black pepper
olive oil

For the sauce
3 tablespoons olive oil
4 medium red onions, peeled and
    sliced as thinly as possible
    into rounds
2 garlic cloves, peeled and cut
    into slivers
2 x 800 g (1.3/4 lb) tins peeled
    plum tomatoes, drained of
    their juices
Maldon salt and freshly ground
    black pepper

extra virgin olive oil
1 bunch rocket leaves

For six

Make the polenta as described on page 63, omitting the butter and Parmesan. When ready, transfer to a large, flat baking tray or plate, and spread out to set.

To make the sauce, heat the oil in a large saucepan or frying pan then add the onions. Reduce the heat and cook the onions until they are very soft. The onions must disappear into the tomato sauce. This will take at least 40 minutes. Some 5 minutes before the end of cooking, add the garlic.

Now add the tomatoes and stir to break them up. Season with salt and pepper and cook slowly, stirring occasionally, for at least 1.1/2 hours. The oil should come to the surface and the sauce will be dark red and extremely thick, with no juice at all.

Preheat the grill or griddle pan. Cut the polenta into individual wedge-shaped slices. Brush lightly with olive oil. Season each side of each slice generously with salt and pepper. Place on the hot grill, turn over when brown and crisp and repeat on the other side.

Serve with the sauce, extra virgin olive oil and a few leaves of rocket.

Grilled Polenta with Mascarpone, Marjoram and Gorgonzola

For the polenta
350 g (12 oz) bramata polenta
1.75-2 litres (3-3.1/2 pints) water
Maldon salt and freshly ground
    black pepper
olive oil

25 g (1 oz) unsalted butter
1 bunch fresh marjoram, leaves
    picked and very roughly
    chopped
225 g (8 oz) Gorgonzola, broken
    into small pieces
100 g (4 oz) mascarpone
Maldon salt and freshly ground
    black pepper

For six

Make the polenta as described on page 63, omitting the butter and Parmesan, then shape and grill the polenta as described on page 64.

Meanwhile, in a small, heavy-bottomed pan, gently heat the butter until it begins to foam. Add half the chopped marjoram and the Gorgonzola. The Gorgonzola should begin to melt very slowly over the low heat.

After a few minutes stir in the mascarpone and season with salt and pepper. Allow the mascarpone and gorgonzola to combine over the heat and serve over the grilled polenta with the remaining marjoram.

Fish and Shellfish

The Italians' approach to fish is instinctively simple yet brilliant. Grilled whole fish – maybe stuffed with fennel herb, rosemary or thyme, its natural juices enhanced by a squeeze of lemon and extra virgin olive oil – is a perfect example.

Going to fresh fish markets in Italy is such a spectacular adventure. Whether in Venice on the east coast, or Piombino just north of Rome, you notice how many varieties there are of every kind of fish, especially unusual fish that you can't even put a name to because they are native to the local waters; tiny baby squid, no bigger than marbles, hand-sized squid that we use to grill whole, very white cuttle fish, seeping their black ink, and sometimes frighteningly large chestnut brown octopuses with their glistening skin.

Supreme quality and freshness are apparent everywhere. We were stunned by beautiful red mullet, luxurious in their boxes, as we were by the colour of the gills of the sea bass – so red, so oxygenated. Fish as fresh as these need only very quick cooking, no matter what the method. Our recipes all follow this rule, searing salmon for minutes on a very hot grill; pan frying squid for seconds flavoured in olive oil.

Traditionally, fish are cooked in their entirety, with the head, eyes and skin intact. You will find roasted whole fish, buried in sea salt, mostly on menus in the south.

Our very successful recipe using turbot simply stuffed with fresh rosemary, packed with coarse sea salt and then roasted, is one of the most popular choices in the restaurant.

In most fish markets in Italy you will find a speciality salt fish stand. These were a revelation to us. You find every size of anchovy, salt cod, dried cod and sardine. The stall holder will even sell you pre-soaked baccalà so that you can cook it immediately.

We have started to cook more baccalà recipes: it is an ingredient steeped in Italian cookery and we have found that people love eating it in the restaurant. Our interest has led us to the salting factories of Norway to look at this fascinating and ancient process for ourselves.

Salted anchovies are an equally important part of our cooking, as we use them like the Italians do, for seasoning, for making Anchovy and Rosemary Sauce (see page 159), and, when you can find the excellent large, red-fleshed ones from Spain, for marinating to serve with bruschetta.

Over the last few years fish has become the primary focus of our main courses in the restaurant. Not only is it delicious to eat but the oils contained in fish and shellfish are far better for us than animal fat.

Spiedini of Monkfish and Scallops (see page 76)

Grilling fish on a skewer is very simple. For the restaurant, we wanted to make this way of cooking more sophisticated, so we chose to use big Scottish scallops and pieces of thick monkfish. The scallop is sweet and rich in taste, while the monkfish has a drier more stringy texture: it's a very successful combination.

As we always think of herbs as an important part of fish flavouring, we use the rosemary stick as a skewer. This imparts a little of its flavour to the fish as it cooks – and the leaves are added to the anchovy in the sauce.

Season the surface very generously with Maldon salt and coarsely ground black pepper. This seals the cut surface of the fish which, when put on the grill, forms a crisp crust. The same technique applies to grilled squid and to seared salmon.

Roasted Red Mullet with Olives, Lemon and Capers (see page 78)

Red mullet is a gutsy fish, with a strong flavour, so it needs strong flavours to complement it. All those ingredients from the south – the olives, capers, tomatoes and lemon – make a perfect marriage. They are not made into a sauce as such, you just let the heat from the frying pan bring them together. We prefer to 'cook' the fish with the ingredients, not just present the fish with the sauce on the side.

Seared Wild Salmon (see page 79)
Wild salmon is more reasonably priced and more commonly available these days because the smoked salmon market now uses farmed salmon, removing the pressure from the wild stocks. To sear the fish, you must cut the fillets like an escalope, cut at an angle to include a thin strip of skin. Sear on both sides on a very hot grill, leaving the centre slightly rare.

Grilled Squid with Chillies (see page 80)
A squid the size of your hand is perfect for grilling; a larger one would be too thick and become rubbery, despite scoring. The scoring, or cross-hatching, on the body of the squid is actually more to do with breaking the skin or flesh tension, so that when you take it off the grill after cooking, it rolls up of its own accord in the shape of a whole squid. In the Mediterranean, squid are usually smaller and are grilled whole. We buy squid fished from the north sea, so scoring is necessary, helping the cooking.

Our fresh red chilli sauce is the perfect complement to the squid. There's a juiciness and flamboyance about fresh chillies. Italians would probably use tiny dried peperoncino and lemon juice to season.

Salt Cod with Artichokes and Porcini (see page 82)
Salt cod, baccalà and stockfish are all different names

for the product of a very ancient industry in which large North Atlantic cod are split open then salted and dried. Italian families tend to buy one big salt cod at Christmas time; it's a rare and expensive treat.

Once salted, cod undergoes a unique transformation; even though you reconstitute it with water, the fish will have completely changed in flavour, texture and consistency. If you have a big enough basin, try to soak a fish whole, then you can very carefully cut it up and use for the recipe. If you have to cut it up before soaking, you may have to use a saw because the preserved fish will be so hard.

Once you have soaked your cod there are a number of ways in which you can use it. We like to make a soup with it, together with tomatoes and potatoes, or a salad, with rocket, chillies, olives and bruschetta; we also stew it, with chickpeas, and grill it and serve it very simply with fresh chilli or tomato sauce. Here we steam it, and put it together with artichokes and porcini.

Whole Turbot with Rosemary Baked in Sea Salt (see page 84)
A fish to be salt-baked must be kept whole. The point about roasting in salt, which is a very Mediterranean thing to do, is that you're encasing the fish, sealing it in the salt crust, which keeps in all the juices and the

true flavour of the fish. If you roasted it without the salt, the skin would break because of the heat, the flesh would dry out a little, and some of the flavour would go into the pan. Choose a fish like turbot or sea bass to bake whole because they are dense with incredible flavour.

Use coarse sea salt for the crust which won't melt in the heat like Maldon.

Grilled Monkfish with Salsa Verde (see page 86)

Monkfish is a beautiful fish, with dense, juicy flesh. Roast a monkfish tail whole on the bone, treating it more like a piece of meat. You can also stud it with herbs as the flesh is so firm. In this recipe the monkfish fillets are scored to butterfly them flat, then grilled very swiftly and serve with a salsa verde.

Whole Grilled and Roasted Sea Bass (see page 88)

There are two methods involved in cooking this delicate and delicious fish whole. Grilling it first seals the skin, and gives it a distinctive flavour; the subsequent roasting of the fish on top of the herbs and wine gives added flavour. We leave the roasted bass in the pan to rest and then serve with the juices poured over.

Pan-Fried Squid with Cannellini Beans (see page 90)

As with grilling, squid need only seconds when pan-frying, and here the flavourings are added during cooking. The sweetness of the squid, plus the zing of the chilli and parsley, complement the creaminess of the cooked beans.

Marinated Salted Anchovies (see page 92)
Anchovies caught in the spring and early summer and then salted by one of the famous salting companies around San Sebastian in Spain, are fantastic because only the best fish are chosen for this process. The colour, shape and flavour are retained as no heat has been applied, and all you have to do is wash the salt off and peel away the fillets.

Salted anchovy is a traditional seasoning for the Italians – like chilli, fennel seeds or dried porcini. It's part of the essential larder, and all over Italy there are market stalls dedicated to selling only salted fish. Buy them here from delicatessens (from large tins by the gram) and keep them in their salt, but only for a couple of days, carefully wrapped in the fridge.

To marinate them after washing, we use freshly squeezed lemon juice and extra virgin olive oil and either parsley, lemon zest, chilli or black pepper. An alternative method uses a white wine with a distinctive flavour like Chardonnay, along with oil, lemon juice and fresh marjoram.

Crab Bruschetta (see page 93)
Freshly cooked crab, simply seasoned and served with bruschetta, is a special summer starter. To complement it, serve a herb salad – perhaps a mixture of fennel herb, basil, mint, wild rocket and sorrel. Dress this with olive oil and lemon juice.

Spiedini of Monkfish and Scallops

12 medium fresh scallops,
   preferably bought live in the
   shell
1 monkfish tail, approximately
   500 g (18 oz) in weight, boned
   and skinned
6 x 15 cm (6 in) rosemary
   branches
Maldon salt and freshly ground
   black pepper
Anchovy and Rosemary Sauce
   (see page 159)
2 lemons, cut into wedges

For six

For each spiedino you need 2 scallops and 2 cubes of monkfish. Pull the leaves off the rosemary stalks, leaving just the tufts at the end. Sharpen the other end into a point.

To prepare the scallops, place them, flat shell side down, on a board. Insert a sharp knife close to the hinge and prise open. Remove the whole scallop from the bottom shell by gently cutting, keeping the blade flat; use a gentle sawing motion. The whole scallop will now be cupped in the top curved half of the shell. Use a tablespoon and carefully scoop out the scallop; trim off the membrane. Wash, then pat dry.

Cut the monkfish into cubes roughly the same size as the scallops. Thread a scallop on first, making sure the rosemary stick goes through the white muscle part and the coral. Next thread on a piece of monkfish, then the other scallop, and finally the other piece of monkfish.

Heat a char-grill or griddle pan. When very hot, season the spiedini generously, then place on the hot pan and grill. Turn over after 3 minutes or when the spiedini no longer stick but have sealed and are brown. Season again, and grill for a further few minutes.

Serve the spiedini with Anchovy and Rosemary Sauce (see page 159) and wedges of lemon.

Roasted Red Mullet with Olives, Lemon and Capers

4 red mullet, approximately 350 g
(12 oz) each in weight, scaled
and cleaned
Maldon salt and freshly ground
black pepper
2 lemons, thinly sliced
60 ml (2 fl oz) olive oil
50 g (2 oz) salted capers, rinsed
of salt, soaked in water and
squeezed dry
50 g (2 oz) Niçoise olives, stones
removed but kept whole
400 g (14 oz) ripe cherry vine
tomatoes, seeds and juices
removed and torn roughly into
pieces
1 bunch fresh marjoram, leaves
picked from stalks
3 garlic cloves, peeled and finely
chopped
75 ml (2.1/2 fl oz) white wine

For four

Preheat the oven to 150°C/300°F/Gas 2.

Season the cavity and the outside of each fish and put 2 slices of lemon inside. Gently heat a roasting pan large enough to contain the fish then brush the surface with olive oil. Place the fish carefully in the pan. Heat over a low heat for 1 minute, just to sear the skin.

Do not turn the fish over as the skin is very thin and it will tear. Roast in the preheated oven for 10 minutes. Remove from the oven and return to the heat. Add the capers, olives, tomatoes, fresh marjoram and finally the garlic. Pour a little olive oil over the fish and a few drops of white wine. Serve with the juices from the pan.

Seared Wild Salmon

1 wild salmon, approximately
    2-3 kg (4.1/2-6.1/2 lb) in weight
Maldon salt and freshly ground
    black pepper
3 lemons

For six to eight

Place the salmon on its side on a board. With a very sharp filleting knife, slice the head off behind the gills. You will expose the main bone. Place one hand on the top side of the salmon to keep it in place and with your other hand cut along the top of the bone, keeping the blade of your knife angled towards the bone, using the finger and thumb of your other hand to lift the side of the salmon away as you cut. You will be cutting through the small fillet bones as you go. Turn the salmon over and repeat the process. You will need to pinbone your two fillets with tweezers. Trim the belly side of the fillets free of fat.

To portion your pieces of salmon, place the fish on its side, skin-side down, on your board. You are aiming to get 6-8 portions altogether, 3-4 from each fillet. Divide the side equally into three by eye, and cut into the salmon at about a 45-degree angle, cutting straight through the skin at the bottom.

Season your pieces of salmon with salt and pepper, and grill skin-side down first on a preheated very hot grill pan or char-grill for about 1 minute until just seared. Turn over and sear the flesh side. Serve with wedges of lemon.

Grilled Squid with Chillies

6 medium squid, no bigger than
    your hand
12 large fresh red chillies, seeded
    and very finely chopped
extra virgin olive oil
Maldon salt and freshly ground
    black pepper
2 tablespoons lemon juice
225 g (8 oz) rocket leaves
3 lemons

For six

Clean the squid by cutting the body open to make a flat piece. Scrape out the guts, keeping the tentacles in their bunches but removing the eyes and mouth. Using a serrated knife, score the inner side of the flattened squid body with parallel lines 1 cm (1/2 in) apart, and then equally apart the other way to make crosshatching.

To make a chilli sauce, put the chopped chillies in a bowl and cover with about 2.5 cm (1 in) of the oil. Season with salt and pepper.

Season the squid (including the tentacles) then place, scored side down, on a very hot grill, and grill for 1-2 minutes. Turn the squid pieces over; they will immediately curl up, by which time they will be cooked.

Mix 6 tablespoons of the oil and the lemon juice, and toss the rocket in this. Arrange a squid body and tentacles on each plate with some of the rocket. Place a little of the chilli sauce on the squid and serve with lemon quarters.

Salt Cod with Artichokes and Porcini

600 g (1 lb 6 oz) salt cod
6 globe artichokes
4 lemons
7 tablespoons olive oil
1 red onion, peeled and chopped
3 garlic cloves, peeled and sliced
Maldon salt and freshly ground
    black pepper
400 g (14 oz) fresh porcini
    mushrooms, brushed clean and
    thickly sliced
1 dried chilli
75 ml (2.1/2 fl oz) white wine
2 tablespoons chopped fresh flat-
    leaf parsley
extra virgin olive oil

For six

Soak the salt cod in cold water for 48 hours if you bought it dried, changing the water at least six times. Soak for only 6 hours if you salted the cod yourself.

To prepare the artichokes, cut off the stalks 2 cm (3/4 in) from the base. Peel or cut away the tough outer leaves until you are left with the pale tender heart. Cut each heart in half (or in quarters if they are large). Scrape away the prickly choke. The artichokes will discolour but this does not alter the taste. Rub with half a lemon to help prevent this.

Heat 2 tablespoons of the olive oil in a thick-bottomed pan. Add the onion and soften over a low flame. Increase the heat, add the artichoke pieces and fry and stir until they have a little colour. Lower the heat, add one-third of the garlic and cook slowly. When the garlic begins to brown add 3 tablespoons water and some salt and pepper. Cover with a lid and cook until the water has evaporated and the chokes are soft. This will take about 10 minutes.

In a separate large pan heat 2 more tablespoons of olive oil. When hot, add the mushrooms and almost immediately one-third of the sliced garlic, frying together over a high heat. Season with the dried chilli, salt and pepper. Squeeze over the juice of half a lemon and remove from the heat.

Remove the cod from the water and pat dry. Cut the fillets in half.

Heat the remaining 3 tablespoons of the olive oil in a large flat pan. Add the rest of the garlic and lightly brown. Carefully place the cod fillets skin side down in the oil and seal for 2 minutes. Add the white wine, season with black pepper, cover the pan with a tightly fitting lid and steam for 6-8 minutes, depending on the thickness of the fillets.

Remove from the heat and allow the cod to cool. Using a spatula, lift the fillets out of the pan, peel off the skin and pull out any bones. Carefully break the cod up into large flakes.

Combine the mushrooms with the artichokes and check for seasoning, then add the cod. Squeeze over the juice of 1 lemon. Finally fold in the chopped parsley and serve with lemon wedges and extra virgin olive oil.

Whole Turbot with Rosemary Baked in Sea Salt

1 turbot head, tail intact,
    approximately 2.25-2.70 kg
    (5-6 lb) in weight, carefully
    gutted
4-5 kg (9-11 lb) natural coarse
    sea salt
1 bunch fresh rosemary
freshly ground black pepper
balsamic vinegar, aged and thick
1 bunch fresh marjoram
extra virgin olive oil
3 lemons

Preheat the oven to
    220°C/425°F/Gas 7.

For six

Use a large baking tray that will snugly hold the turbot. Cover the bottom with a layer of salt, and place the turbot on the salt. Push the rosemary into the cavity and completely cover the fish with the remainder of the salt, about 1.5 cm (3/4 in) thick. Do not worry if the head and tail protrude. Sprinkle the surface of the salt very lightly with a little water – use a few tablespoons.

Place in the preheated oven and bake for 25-35 minutes. After 20 minutes test to see if it is done: push a cooking fork or the point of a small sharp knife through the crust until you touch the centre spine bone, approximately where the fish is fattest under its mound of salt. Bring the fork up and touch on your lips or on the inside of your wrist. If it feels hot it's done, perhaps even overdone; if it's warm, take the fish out of the oven and leave it to rest for a few minutes before cracking the crust.

Allow to cool for 5 minutes then crack open the salt crust. Carefully remove as much of the salt as possible. You may find the thick skin of the turbot will stick to the salt. Peel away the skin and lift out the fillets onto serving plates.

Serve at room temperature, with coarsely ground black pepper, a few dribbles of balsamic vinegar, fresh marjoram leaves, extra virgin olive oil and lemon wedges.

Grilled Monkfish with Salsa Verde

1 monkfish tail, head removed,
    approximately 1.4 kg (3 lb) in
    weight
2 lemons
Maldon salt and freshly ground
    black pepper
olive oil
Salsa Verde (see page 160)

For six

Place the monkfish tail on a board, skin side up. Holding the top of the tail with one hand, grab the skin at the neck and pull it back towards you with your other hand so that it peels away from the body and comes right off. It is easier to grip using a cloth. Two fillets on either side of the bone will be exposed. Carefully cut them away from the bone using a sharp knife.

Remove the tough membrane from the fillets by placing them cut side up and the tail end nearest you. With your fingers holding the tail end of the membrane, insert the knife, sloping it down and away from the flesh, towards the membrane and cut all along, moving forward at an angle until the membrane is removed.

Trim the fillet so that you are left with the white flesh.

Cut the fillet in half. Place one hand flat over the top of the fat end of the fillet to hold it in place. With a sharp knife cut into the fillet horizontally about three-quarters of the way through so that it butterflies out. Score it lightly with the knife. The tail end fillet needs to be scored slightly deeper at the fan end with the scores made more shallow as they go back towards the tail.

Heat the grill to very hot.

Place the butterflied fillets on a plate, squeeze the lemon juice over them and season with salt and pepper and a little olive oil. Grill for 3-4 minutes on either side.

Serve with a wedge of lemon and Salsa Verde (see page 160).

Whole Grilled and Roasted Sea Bass

1 whole sea bass, approximately
    2.25 kg (5 lb) in weight, scaled
    and cleaned
2 tablespoons fennel seeds
Maldon salt and coarsely ground
    black pepper
5 tablespoons olive oil
2 lemons, sliced
a few parsley stalks
2 fresh fennel bulbs, trimmed and
    sliced
juice of 1 lemon
75 ml (2.1/2 fl oz) white wine

Preheat the oven to
    190°C/375°F/Gas 5.

Preheat the grill.

For four to six

Put half the fennel seeds and some salt and pepper inside the cavity of the fish, brush the skin with a little olive oil and grill for about 5 minutes on each side until the skin is lightly charred.

Place half the lemon slices, parsley stalks, fennel slices and the remaining fennel seeds in a large ovenproof dish, lay the fish on top and cover with the remaining lemon and fennel. Pour over the lemon juice, remaining olive oil and the white wine, and bake in the oven for about 30 minutes, or until the flesh is firm to the touch.

Serve either hot or cold with a Salsa Verde (see page 160).

Pan-Fried Squid with Cannellini Beans

For the cannellini beans

250 g (9 oz) dried cannellini
    beans

1 tablespoon bicarbonate of soda

1 head garlic

a handful of fresh sage leaves

6 tablespoons extra virgin olive
    oil

Maldon salt and freshly ground
    black pepper

1.8 kg (4 lb) fresh whole squid,
    7-10 cm (3-4 in) long, cleaned,
    tentacles intact

Maldon salt and freshly ground
    black pepper

extra virgin olive oil

2 tablespoons dried oregano

3 small dried chillies

2 garlic cloves, peeled and finely
    chopped

3 lemons (1 cut in half for
    squeezing)

3 handfuls fresh Italian flat-leaf
    parsley, roughly chopped

For six

Soak the beans overnight in a generous amount of water with the bicarbonate of soda.

Preheat the oven to 200°C/400°F/Gas 6.

Drain the beans well and place them in a baking dish. Add the garlic, sage and enough water to come three-quarters up the sides of the baking dish. Pour in the olive oil to cover the beans. Cover the dish with foil and make a small hole in the centre with the point of a knife to allow steam to escape.

Place the baking dish in the preheated oven and cook until the beans are very tender, about 45 minutes – although the cooking time will vary according to the quality of the beans. The liquid will evaporate, and the beans will become very tender. Season generously with salt and pepper, and warm through gently while you prepare the squid.

Clean the squid as described on page 80.

Use a large thick-bottomed frying pan and heat until very hot. Lightly brush with olive oil and, before the oil begins to burn, add the squid. Immediately scatter over the oregano, crumbled dried chillies, garlic and a little salt and pepper. Turn each squid over and brown the other side – this will take a matter of seconds.

Add the juice of half a lemon and half the chopped parsley, stir and remove from the heat.

Place the seasoned cannellini beans on a large platter, scatter with the remaining chopped parsley, and drizzle over some extra virgin olive oil. Place the fried squid and their juices over the beans and serve with the remaining lemons cut into quarters.

Marinated Salted Anchovies

2 kg (4.1/2 lb) salted anchovies
Maldon salt and freshly ground
   black pepper
2 tablespoons dried chilli,
   crumbled
1 bunch fresh flat-leaf parsley,
   finely chopped
juice of 4 lemons
250 ml (8 fl oz) extra virgin olive
   oil

For six

Wash the anchovies well to remove all the salt, then fillet them: pull each fillet gently away from the spine, discard the fins and tails. Wash thoroughly and hang over the side of a bowl to drain.

In a serving dish arrange a layer of anchovies silver side up, side by side, not overlapping, and sprinkle with black pepper, chilli and parsley. Pour over some lemon juice and a little olive oil. Repeat the layers, making sure that the top layer is covered with oil and lemon.

Leave to marinate for about 1/2 hour before serving with either salad or bruschetta (see page 132).

Crab Bruschetta

3 live crabs, approximately
   1-1.4 kg (2-3 lb) each in weight
Maldon salt and freshly ground
   black pepper
juice of 2 lemons
6 tablespoons extra virgin olive
   oil
4 medium fresh chillies, seeded
   and chopped
6 slices sourdough bruschetta
   (see page 132)
1 small bunch green fennel herb,
   roughly chopped
6 lemon wedges
a handful rocket leaves

For six

Put each crab in its own large saucepan of cold water. Add 50 g (2 oz) salt to each pan, cover, and very slowly bring to the boil. The crabs are cooked when the water reaches boiling point. Remove the crabs from the pans, drain and leave to cool.

Break each crab open by pulling away the upper body shell. Scrape out the brown meat and put into a bowl. Break the claws and legs from the body, crack and pick out the white meat, keeping the pieces as large as possible. Place in a separate bowl.

Mix two-thirds of the lemon juice with the oil and chillies, then season. Add to the bowl of white meat. Season the brown meat with salt, pepper and the remaining lemon juice only.

Prepare the bruschetta as described on page 132. Cover half of each bruschetta generously with brown crab meat and half with white meat. Sprinkle over the fennel, and serve with a lemon wedge and rocket leaves.

Meat, Poultry and Game

In Italy you always find simple roasted and grilled meats on the menu. The beef of Tuscany, the pork of Emilia Romagna, where the Parmesan cheese is made and the by-product is fed to the pigs, the young lamb and kid from Rome. Ducks, chickens and guinea fowl are still kept by almost every Italian household with a patch of garden or small farm. They are usually fed vegetable scraps and maize corn, they wander freely and subsequently taste amazing.

The Italians are very particular and appreciative of the flavour of their meat which is usually cooked simply with herbs, garlic and wine. We have developed most of our meat and game recipes from dishes eaten there.

For our programme we were lucky to watch wild pheasants being cooked in a very special way at the Felsina wine estate in Chianti classico. That kind of experience inspires us when cooking in the restaurant. It's how we came to match to distinct flavours of pancetta and prosciutto with game and poultry; the strong flavour of Coppa with pork; the unique flavour of balsamic vinegar with our steamed and roasted duck.

We spend a lot of time talking to butchers and game dealers, working with them to broaden their range of produce. This allows us to cook with the most suitable ingredient for any given recipe. We love the chance to use older, free-range hens for the Bollito Misto and find different varieties of duck – certain types are perfect for boiling while other breeds roast more successfully. Without working with our suppliers this would be impossible.

You will notice from our selection of recipes in this chapter that wine plays a large part in our meat cooking. Regionality of wine and food is very important. Not only would a Tuscan not drink a Piedmont wine with his native dish, he would not cook with it either and nor do we.

We love to cook with wine that we plan to drink with the dish, particularly grouse and partridge, usually adding it at the end of roasting so that it doesn't lose its character. However, when we cook with robust wines like Marsala, we use them from the beginning, not only to add flavour but also because they don't change enormously during cooking.

Pan-Roasted Guinea Fowl Wrapped in Prosciutto (see page 102)
Game cookery is something that we love. Here whole guinea fowl are covered with slices of prosciutto to flavour the skin. The birds are slow-cooked on top of the stove with garlic, sage, rosemary and some Marsala. When they are ready, a little milk is added to the juices to make a simple sauce.

Roast Guinea Fowl Stuffed with Pomegranate and Thyme (see page 104)

Pomegranates grow all over southern Italy. Their sour-sweet flavour here complements the guinea fowl, married with the pungency of fresh thyme and the sweetness of Marsala.

Grilled Pigeon Marinated in Valpolicella di Classico with Rosemary (see page 106)

We use Bresse pigeons, which are plump, organically fed and reared to a certain size. (Don't use a wild wood pigeon, as it will be too tough.) These pigeons cook very quickly; spatchcock them by taking out the breast bone, leaving only the legs on the bone. Put briefly into the marinade made with a fresh, young wine such as Valpolicella.

Summer Bollito Misto (see page 108)

We have been cooking Bollito Misto since the River Cafe opened. Bollito plays a very special part in Italian cuisine, and it is historically served at New Year. Each ingredient represents different benefits for the coming year: the meats symbolise health, the lentils wealth and the mostarda di Cremona good spirits.

In this recipe we have changed the ingredients to make it lighter. We use a large, mature hen – not a roasting chicken – Barbary ducks and cotechino, and in the summer we cook green vegetables such as spinach and chard in the chicken broth at the end.

Steamed and Roasted Duck (see page 110)
This recipe is interesting because the double cooking is oriental in origin. The duck is steamed first to allow the fat to run out, and is then roasted to crisp the skin and cook the flesh, which falls off the bone on serving. Putting balsamic vinegar on the skin while roasting gives it a distinctive flavour.

Pan-Roasted Chicken Stuffed with Mascarpone and Prosciutto (see page 112)
In this recipe a pocket between the flesh and skin of a boned breast and bit of leg is filled with mascarpone, herbs and a slice of prosciutto. The flavour of the prosciutto permeates the chicken flesh and the cheese melts, moisturising the meat. It also forms a natural sauce, which you deglaze at the end with a little wine.

Braised Pheasant with Cabbage (see page 114)
In Italy you find pheasants everywhere during the season. They are often pot roasted and in Tuscany they cook them with Chianti and tomatoes. Knowing the age of a game bird is important because an older bird will need to be cooked for much longer in the liquid. In this recipe we roast the birds first, then braise them slowly with pancetta, wine and cabbage.

Roast Pheasant with Quince and Sage (see page 116)
For roasting, we like to choose young hen pheasants, which are usually quite small, rounder, with more flesh than the cocks. Pheasant is hugely complemented by fruit, and quince, with its distinctive strong taste, is in season at the same time.

Roast Partridge Wrapped in Pancetta and Stuffed with Thyme (see page 117)
Instead of lard or bacon on top of a game bird we use pancetta or prosciutto, and simply stuff it with branches of thyme and sage. The strong taste of the game can take these flavours.

It is important to allow the bird to rest before serving.

Loin of Pork (or Wild Boar) Wrapped in Coppa di Parma (see page 118)
Wild boar is common in Italy, and they also have excellent pork. In this country they are now cross-breeding pig with wild boar for a pork with a gamey flavour. As this is still quite hard to find, we use organic pigs which have a distinctive flavour. They also have a natural marbling of fat. Always ask your butcher about the provenance of his meat and try to buy organic whenever possible.

Here, the boned loin is wrapped in freshly sliced coppa di Parma (shoulder of pork cured in the same way as prosciutto di Parma). This has a smoky flavour, and introduces a juniper taste, as well as keeping the meat moist. This is a Christmas dish, so we roast whole chestnuts in the pan with the meat.

Roast Spring Lamb Stuffed and Wrapped with Rosemary (see page 120)
The Italians love the intense perfume of rosemary. We use it to marinate lamb and in this recipe the whole leg of lamb is wrapped in it.

Pan-Roasted Guinea Fowl Wrapped in Prosciutto

1 guinea fowl, approximately 1 kg
    (2.1/2 lb) in weight
Maldon salt and coarsely ground
    black pepper
5 slices prosciutto, approximately
    300 g (10 oz) in weight
2 tablespoons olive oil
50 g (2 oz) unsalted butter
4 garlic cloves, peeled
6 leaves fresh sage
1 branch rosemary
120 ml (4 fl oz) dry Marsala
120 ml (4 fl oz) Chicken Broth
    (see page 22)
150 ml (5 fl oz) milk

For two

Season the inside of the guinea fowl with salt and pepper. Place the slices of prosciutto over the breasts and legs and secure with string.

Heat the oil and butter together in a saucepan. When hot add the bird and brown gently on all sides. Add the garlic, sage and rosemary and cook together for just 1-2 minutes. Take out the bird and drain off excess oil and butter. Return the bird to the pan and add the Marsala. Scrape up the juices and herbs to combine, then add the stock. Bring to the boil, lower the heat and simmer gently with the lid on for 45-60 minutes. The bird is cooked when the juices run clear. Remove the bird and untie the string.

Add the milk to the pan and stir to make a simple sauce. Adjust the seasoning.

Cut the bird into halves. Serve the breast whole with the leg and some of the crisp prosciutto, with the pan juices poured over.

Roast Guinea Fowl Stuffed with Pomegranate and Thyme

2 guinea fowl, approximately
   1.5 kg (3.1/4 lb) each in weight
4 fresh ripe pomegranates
100 g (4 oz) unsalted butter
Maldon salt and freshly ground
   black pepper
2 garlic cloves, peeled
1 bunch fresh thyme
250 g (9 oz) pancetta, thinly
   sliced
150 ml (5 fl oz) red wine

For four

Preheat the oven to 220°C/425°F/Gas 7.

Cut each of the pomegranates in half and scoop out the flesh and seeds from the shells of two of them. Squeeze the juice from the remaining two, using an orange juice squeezer.

Wipe the cavity of the birds to make sure they are clean and dry. Spread inside generously with butter and season with salt and pepper. Stuff each bird with the pomegranate seeds, 1 garlic clove, the thyme and 1 slice pancetta. Butter the breasts of each bird and then cover with the remaining slices of pancetta. Tie this on securely with string. Season the outside of the birds with salt and pepper.

Heat the remaining butter in an ovenproof dish large enough to hold the guinea fowl, and quickly brown the birds on each side. Pour in half the wine and let it bubble for 1-2 minutes to reduce slightly. Place the dish in the preheated oven, the birds breast side up, and roast for 25-30 minutes. Turn the birds over and baste with 2-3 spoons of the squeezed pomegranate juice, then continue to roast for a further 15 minutes. Test for doneness: one leg away from the body – the juices should flow clear and there should be no blood.

Return the birds to the oven, breast side up, add the remainder of the wine and roast for a further

5 minutes, or until the birds are cooked. Remove from the oven. Place the guinea fowl on a warm serving plate. Untie the string and discard the pancetta.

Skim the excess fat from the roasting pan and place on a medium heat. Add the remainder of the pomegranate juice and stir to combine with the wine and juices from the birds. Reduce for a few minutes, the sauce should become syrupy. Season, then pour the juice over the birds and serve with the stuffing.

Grilled Pigeon Marinated in Valpolicella di Classico with Rosemary

6 Bresse pigeons
Maldon salt and coarsely ground
    black pepper
grated zest of 2 lemons
6 garlic cloves, peeled and sliced
1 bunch fresh rosemary, leaves
    picked from the stalks
500 ml (17 fl oz) Valpolicella di
    Classico
3 tablespoons olive oil

For six

To flatten the birds, using a large knife, make a cut down either side of the backbone and remove. Now use a small knife and carefully cut the body carcass and breast bones away from the meat. Spread each bird out flat, and place in a large flat dish. Season with salt and pepper, scatter over the lemon zest, garlic and rosemary, and add the Valpolicella and olive oil. Turn over in the marinade and leave for 1 hour.

Preheat the char-grill or griddle pan to medium hot. Remove the birds from the marinade; strain and keep the liquid.

Place the birds on the grill, skin side down, and cook for 3-4 minutes, positioning the legs of each bird, which take longer to cook, on the hottest part of the grill. The breast should remain slightly pink. Turn and cook for a further 5-10 minutes.

Spoon a little of the marinade over each bird in the final few minutes. Remove from the grill, and spoon a little more marinade over each bird whilst they rest.

Summer Bollito Misto

2 Barbary ducks, approximately
   1.5 kg (3.1/2 lb) each in weight
1 free-range boiling hen,
   approximately 1.5 kg (3.1/2 lb)
   in weight
1 pre-cooked cotechino
Maldon salt and freshly ground
   black pepper
2 heads celery, hearts and leaves
12 organic baby summer carrots
1 bunch fresh thyme
8 bay leaves
6 garlic cloves
1 large bunch Swiss chard,
   washed and stems chopped off
1 tablespoon whole black
   peppercorns

For six

Put the hen into a saucepan large enough to hold it. Add water to cover, the celery stalks, 3 garlic cloves (unpeeled), 3-4 sprigs thyme, 2 carrots, the whole black peppercorns and the remaining fresh bay leaves. Bring to the boil and simmer for about 1.3/4 hours.

At the same time, fill a saucepan large enough to hold the ducks with enough water to keep them completely submerged. Bring the water to the boil.

Season the inside of the duck cavities with salt and pepper and insert some celery leaves, a couple of the carrots, 1 sprig thyme, 1 bay leaf and 1 garlic clove. Wrap each duck in a clean tea towel and tie securely with string. This holds the ducks together during the long cooking time and the cloth helps to absorb some of the duck fat.

Place the ducks in the boiling water and weight down to keep them submerged. Simmer for 1.1/2 hours. Remove, drain well and cool before unwrapping.

30 minutes before serving
After the hen and ducks have been cooking for 1.1/4 hours, place the cotechino in a separate saucepan of boiling water and cook for about 30 minutes.

20 minutes before serving
With a ladle, transfer into a separate saucepan enough

of the stock that the hen has been cooking in to cook the vegetables. Pass it through a sieve. Bring to the boil and put in the Swiss chard leaves and the remaining carrots. Cook for 10 minutes. Remove and keep hot.

To serve

Test the chickens for doneness by pulling a leg away from the body; it should come away easily if cooked. Remove from the pan and strain. Reserve the remaining stock but discard the remaining vegetables and herbs. Unwrap the ducks.

Cut 1 cm (1/2 in) slices from the breast and leg of the chickens, and from the ducks, using both white and brown meat. Cut the cotechino or zampone into 1 cm (1/2 in) slices at an angle.

Arrange the meats on a large warm serving plate and pour over some of the seasoned chicken stock. Arrange the carrots and Swiss chard around the meats and serve the meats with Tarragon Sauce and Horseradish Sauce (see pages 159 and 158) and a bottled relish, mostarda di Cremona or mustard fruits.

Steamed and Roasted Duck

3 Barbary ducks, approximately
   1.5 kg (3.1/4 lb) each in weight
Maldon salt and freshly ground
   black pepper
8 new garlic cloves, peeled
3 organic lemons, halved
4 celery stalks, with their leaves,
   roughly chopped
4 small organic carrots, scrubbed
   and roughly chopped
1 teaspoon fennel seeds
   (optional)
6 tablespoons young balsamic
   vinegar
15 g (1/2 oz) unsalted butter

For six

Preheat the oven to 200°C/400°F/Gas 6.

Trim the neck skin from the ducks and remove all fat from the cavities. Using a fork, prick the duck skin in places where the fat deposits are thickest. Rub the whole ducks inside and out with sea salt.

Pulse-chop the garlic, 2 of the lemons, the celery stalks and leaves and the carrots. Add salt, pepper and fennel seeds if using. Push this mixture inside each bird. Squeeze the remaining lemon over the birds, and set them breast side up in a roasting tray on a rack. Half fill the tray with boiling water. Completely cover the ducks with foil, wrapping it round the edge of the tray to make an airtight seal. Steam-bake for 1 hour. Remove the foil, and pour away the water. Pour half the balsamic vinegar over the ducks and season the breasts. Turn the oven temperature up to 225°C/425°F/ Gas 7. Roast for a further 15 minutes to brown the breasts, then turn the ducks over. Reduce the oven temperature to 200°C/400°F/Gas 6, and roast for a further 45-60 minutes. The skin should be dark brown and crisp, the flesh coming away from the bones.

Rest for 5 minutes before cutting the birds in half along the breastbone. Deglaze the roasting tray with the butter, remaining balsamic vinegar and 1 tablespoon of lemon juice. Pour over each serving of duck and stuffing.

Pan-Roasted Chicken Stuffed with Mascarpone and Prosciutto

3 free-range or corn-fed chickens, approximately 1.2 kg (2.1/2 lb) each in weight, boned and cut in half or 6 chicken breasts with the short part of the wing joint and skin left on and the thigh boned out and skin on
2 tablespoons very finely chopped rosemary leaves
12 tablespoons mascarpone cheese
Maldon salt and freshly ground black pepper
6 large slices prosciutto San Daniele
4 tablespoons olive oil
2 lemons

For six

Preheat the oven to 230°C/450°F/Gas 8.

To bone the chicken, place the chicken, breast side up, on a board. With a sharp boning knife, cut along the breast bone, then guide the knife, cutting between breast and carcass on one side, down to the leg joint. You have to cut the wishbone in half to divide the breast at its centre. Crack the leg bone at the joint away from the carcass so that it lies flat on the board. With the knife, carefully cut around the joint, separating the whole on one side from its carcass. Repeat this with the other side.

Snip the wing tips from the wings, leaving the bone in the short part of the wing. To remove the bones from the legs, flatten out your chicken half skin down. Using the leg bones as a guide, cut as close to them on either side as possible, and then insert the tip of the knife and prise up one bone, cutting as you do so. It is always difficult near the joint between thigh and drumstick, but you must try not to cut the skin which ultimately will hold your stuffing. Trim any flabby bits of skin and cut away any pieces of fat.

With your hands gently separate the skin of the chicken breast and thigh from the meat, creating pockets for the stuffing. Mix the rosemary with the mascarpone, and season with salt and pepper.

Using 1 slice prosciutto per chicken breast, divide it into two pieces – one roughly the size of the surface of the thigh and the other the size of the chicken breast. Stuff the prosciutto in between the skin and meat where you have made your pockets; the prosciutto should make a second skin inside the pockets. Place 1 large tablespoon of the mascarpone mixture into each pocket between the prosciutto and the flesh of the chicken.

Heat the oil in a large ovenproof frying pan or roasting tray and brown the pieces quickly on both sides. Put into the preheated oven and roast for about 15-20 minutes. Test for doneness by pulling the leg joint away from the body. If the juices run pink, cook a little longer.

Remove the pan from the oven and, over a medium heat, add the lemon juice. It will immediately combine with the mascarpone and chicken juices. Turn the chicken to coat it with the sauce, and serve.

Braised Pheasant with Cabbage

2 pheasants, approximately
675 g-1.1 kg (1.1/2-2.1/2 lb)
each in weight
1 small Savoy cabbage, shredded
and blanched
2 tablespoons olive oil
100 g (4 oz) pancetta, cut into
matchsticks
2 garlic cloves, peeled and thinly
sliced
175 ml (6 fl oz) white wine
300 ml (10 fl oz) Chicken Broth
(see page 22)

For four

Preheat the oven to 230°C/450°F/Gas 8.

Heat the oil in a saucepan just large enough to hold the pheasants. Over a medium-high heat brown the pheasants well all over, one at a time. Remove from the saucepan and place in a roasting pan. Roast in the preheated oven for 20 minutes, then let the birds relax for 5 minutes. They will still be quite pink.

Add the pancetta to the saucepan and fry until brown. Add the sliced garlic and cook for a minute. Pour in the wine and boil to reduce. Now add the cabbage and sufficient stock to combine.

With a large knife cut the birds into halves through the breast bone and then separate the legs. Place the pheasant pieces in the pancetta and cabbage mixture. Cover with a tight-fitting lid. Cook very gently together over a low heat for 40 minutes.

Roast Pheasant with Quince and Sage

3 young hen pheasants
Maldon salt and freshly ground
    black pepper
3 quinces, peeled and sliced
1 bunch fresh sage
100 g (4 oz) unsalted butter
6 slices pancetta affumicata
2 tablespoons olive oil
300 ml (10 fl oz) red wine
    (Chianti Classico)
5 garlic cloves, peeled
2 tablespoons Quince Cheese
    (see page 161)

For six

Preheat the oven to 220°C/425°F/Gas 7.

Wipe the cavity of each bird and season with salt and pepper. Toss the quince and some of the sage leaves in a little of the butter, then place one-third of this plus a knob of butter inside each pheasant. Place the slices of pancetta over the breast of each bird and tie in place.

Heat the oil in a roasting tray. Brown the pheasants on the underside and around the legs. Add the garlic cloves, a little butter and half of the wine, and allow the wine to reduce for 3 minutes. Place the tray in the preheated oven, with the birds breast side up, and roast for 35-40 minutes. Test for doneness by pulling a leg away from the body. If the meat is pink, and you like pheasant rare, it is ready.

Remove from the oven. Pull the softened quince from inside the cavities into the pan juices and place the pheasants on a warm plate to rest. Return the roasting tray to heat, and skim off any surplus fat. Add the remaining sage leaves and soften for 1 minute. Add the remaining wine and quince cheese, stir to combine with the roasting juices and quince, and allow it to reduce to form a sauce. Taste for seasoning.

Cut each pheasant into halves and serve with the quince sauce and sage leaves.

Roast Partridge Wrapped in Pancetta and Stuffed with Thyme

6 partridges, plucked and cleaned
6 fresh thyme branches
Maldon salt and freshly ground
    black pepper
18 slices pancetta affumicata
2 tablespoons olive oil
300 ml (10 fl oz) Chianti Classico
50 g (2 oz) butter

For six

Preheat the oven to 230°C/450°F/Gas 8.

Stuff the partridge with the thyme branches, and season inside and out. Place 3 slices pancetta across the breast and legs of each bird and tie in place with string.

In a large roasting pan heat the olive oil and brown the birds on all sides on top of the stove. When they are sealed, roast in the hot oven for 10 minutes. Remove the birds from the pan and leave to rest in a warm place, breast side down, cavity facing up.

Deglaze the roasting pan with the Chianti and the butter, season, allow the juices to reduce by half then pour over the birds.

Loin of Pork (or Wild Boar) Wrapped in Coppa di Parma

1.8-2.25 kg (4-5 lb) boned loin of young organic pork (or wild boar), rind and most of the fat removed

450 g (1 lb) coppa di Parma, thinly sliced

4-5 garlic cloves, peeled and finely sliced

3-4 sprigs fresh rosemary, leaves picked from stalks

Maldon salt and freshly ground black pepper

200 g (7 oz) unsalted butter

500 g (1 lb 2 oz) fresh whole chestnuts, scored

1 bottle Amerone di Valpolicella

Preheat the oven to 220°C/425°F/Gas 7.

For six

With a sharp knife, make small incisions all over the loin of pork, following the grain of the meat. Into each incision, insert a sliver of garlic, a sprig of rosemary, salt and pepper.

Cut a sheet of greaseproof paper large enough to wrap around the loin. Lay the slices of coppa slightly overlapping over the whole sheet. Place the loin in the centre, roll up and tie with string.

Melt half the butter in a heavy-bottomed saucepan until it begins to foam. Seal the loin on all sides, turning it over in the butter until it is browned. Add the chestnuts and about a third of the wine. Press a large knob of butter on top of the meat and roast for 25-45 minutes, depending on the size of the loin.

Turn the meat a few times during the cooking and add more wine if necessary. Test for doneness by pressing the loin – if it gives gently it will still be quite rare and will need more time. The meat should be almost firm to touch. When cooked, remove the loin from the oven, cut away the string, and leave to rest while you finish the sauce.

Skim any fat from the roasting pan. Add the remainder of the wine and cook until the juices are thick and have combined with some of the chestnuts. Cut thick slices and pour over the juices. Serve with the chestnuts.

Roast Spring Lamb Stuffed and Wrapped with Rosemary

1 leg of lamb, approximately
   1.8-2.25 kg (4-5 lb) in weight
10 branches soft summer
   rosemary, about 10 cm (4 in)
   long
5 large garlic cloves, peeled
Maldon salt and freshly ground
   black pepper
3 tablespoons olive oil
175 ml (6 fl oz) white wine
1 lemon

For six

Preheat the oven to 220°C/425°F/Gas 7.

Carefully remove the thigh bone from the leg of lamb, keeping the shank bone and the leg intact. Ask your butcher to do this if necessary.

Remove the leaves from two of the rosemary branches and pound together with the garlic, salt and pepper until you have a thick paste.

Lay your leg of lamb on a board and season the cavity where the bone was removed. Generously smear the rosemary and garlic paste all over the inside surface, pushing the mixture down towards the inside of the shank bone.

Roll up the lamb lengthways and tie with string at regular intervals to secure the shape of the leg and retain the stuffing.

Place the 8 remaining rosemary branches along the length of the leg on all sides and tie to secure with more string. The legs should be practically completely covered. Season the outside with salt and pepper and rub generously with some of the olive oil.

Heat the roasting tin, and add the remainder of the olive oil. Place the lamb into the hot tin and seal briefly on all sides. Roast in a preheated oven for 20 minutes then turn the leg over and pour in the wine. Reduce the oven temperature to 200°C/400°F/Gas 6 and roast for a further hour. Turn and baste the lamb with the juices from time to time.

Remove the leg from the roasting pan and leave to rest before carving. Spoon off excess fat and remove the rosemary branches. Add the juice of the lemon to the pan. Stir into the meat juices to make a simple sauce, season and pour over the carved lamb.

Vegetables and Salads

Vegetables form a very important part of our cooking. In Italy vegetables are cooked simply but very carefully; the seasons dictate availability. The special quality and taste of individual varieties is what interests us, as is the proper growing of plants in their natural, organic way with the correct amount of natural sunshine and water.

Seeing the enormous variety of vegetables in the markets in Italy has spurred us on to encourage market gardeners here to try growing some of these previously unknown Mediterranean vegetables.

Their work has been such a success that cavolo nero, the black, bitter winter cabbage of Florence, is now available in supermarkets as are a wide variety of pumpkins and squashes. Rocket salad, trevise, cima di rape and Swiss chard also grow easily here and the difference in quality of freshly picked vegetables as opposed to those that have travelled across Europe for days is very obvious in the cooking and eating.

In the programme we hope to excite you with ideas for salads – such as the raw zucchini with Parmesan, or the unusual combination of boiled lemon and artichokes in a salad with almonds, honey and thyme.

Wood roasting is a method we use over and over for vegetables in every season. Your domestic oven will roast in virtually the same way. Discovering how roasting at high temperatures intensifies flavours has led us to experiment, starting simply with the sweet cherry tomatoes on the vine, to more complicated 'al fornos' such as potato, pancetta and trevise in which the sliced potatoes slowly take up the flavours of the pancetta, rosemary, garlic and bitter trevise.

Pumpkins and squashes we roast very quickly. The initial generous seasoning with herbs and spices and the way that the vegetables are cut is what gives our recipes their particular character.

In Italy, green vegetables (and there are so many varieties like spinach, Swiss chard, cicoria and cima di rape) are all blanched simply but – we cannot stress this enough – carefully, and then used as antipasta. For us there is nothing more delicious than eating a plate of these blanched vegetables when they have been beautifully seasoned, and that means the best extra virgin olive oil, coarsely ground black pepper, freshly squeezed lemon juice and Maldon sea salt.

Bruschetta with Garlic and Extra Virgin Olive Oil (see page 132)

Use sourdough bread that has an open texture. Sourdough bread will last for up to 2 weeks. The starter from one batch of bread can be used for the next. A bakery in Puglia uses a sourdough starter dating back to 1945.

Bruschetta with Squashed Tomatoes, Dried Oregano and Chilli (see page 132)
Use a combination of ripe yellow and red tomatoes. Choose large tomatoes so that there is plenty of juice to push into the toast.

Bruschetta with Baked Borlotti Beans (see page 134)
In speciality grocery shops in Italy, you can find two or three different grades of borlotti beans, including the really plump, fabulous ones, known as borlotti di Lamon. Here you can find dried borlotti in health-food shops and Italian shops; you can also buy them canned. In the summer they are available fresh in their pods.

The baking method for the beans is based on an old-fashioned technique. In this method, the beans were put into a large glass Chianti bottle; water, oil and sage were added, and the neck was stuffed with straw to allow steam to escape. The bottle was put over a fire and the beans were slowly cooked until the water evaporated. The principle in the oven is the same: as the beans slowly cook, they absorb the flavourings and water as well as a bit of the oil. The final result is a bean that has absorbed the olive oil, and all you need to do is season.

Bruschetta with Mashed Broad Beans (see page 135)
This is a wonderful recipe when broad beans are very young and tender. Smashed with mint and garlic, there

is no cooking, just blending together in the way you make pesto, adding cheese at the end.

Bruschetta with Fresh Porcini (see page 136)
The porcini season begins in September and October and finishes when there is a hard frost. Choose big, firm ones and slice them through the stems and caps. Season with dried chilli to complement their unique flavour and add lemon juice at the end of cooking.

Bruschetta with Cima di Rape (see page 138)
Cima di rape is the flowering shoots and leaves of a variety of the turnip family. It has a strong individual taste and is best blanched then tossed with the new season's olive oil, and served on bruschetta with lemon juice and black pepper. Castellucio lentils are delicious combined with cima di rape and make a more substantial dish.

Wood-Roasted Cherry Vine Tomatoes (see page 139)
Keep the tomatoes on the vine while roasting and serve them in bunches – they look great. It's important to wash the stems thoroughly before cooking as they may have been sprayed.

Wood-Roasted Asparagus (see page 139)
The asparagus cooks very quickly. Use Niçoise olives as they are the nearest to the small, purple olives you find preserved in brine in Tuscany.

Wood-Roasted Peppers (see page 140)

Roasted red and yellow peppers go well together. Try to find dried wild oregano on its stalks with its flowers – the flavour from oregano dried in this way is intense and complements the sweetness of the peppers.

Wood-Roasted Zucchini (see page 140)

Small zucchini should just be cut in half; bigger ones should be sliced lengthwise into 2 cm (1 in) batons. Always scrape out the seeded centre of large zucchini as they have a bitter taste.

Wood-Roasted Pumpkin (see page 141)

Onion squash has firm orange flesh that is ideal for wood roasting. Leave the skin on the pumpkin because as it cooks it caramelises, and tastes divine. Season with ground coriander seeds, garlic, salt and pepper; or dried oregano, garlic and chilli; or thyme smashed with garlic, salt and pepper.

Only drizzle on a little olive oil when roasting. Serve with roast meats and birds, or use in risotto and soups.

Wood-Roasted Celeriac (see page 141)

Buy small celeriac with green shoots on the top and tangled roots. Large ones often have holes in the middle and have lost their flavour. Cut in wedges to roast and flavour with thyme and garlic.

Wood-Roasted Potato and Trevise (see page 142)

The combination of bitter trevise, sweet pancetta and rosemary make a perfect combination with sliced waxy potatoes such as Roseval. The potato mixture is layered in a baking dish and roasted slowly in the wood oven.

Wood-Roasted Jerusalem Artichokes (see page 143)

Jerusalem artichokes are small, knobbly and difficult to peel. They also cook quickly. They have a very distinctive flavour of their own, but are complemented by woody herbs like thyme and rosemary. Serve with other roast vegetables. You can also use this recipe with Ratte or Pink Fir Apple potatoes, or with sweet potatoes.

Raw Zucchini Salad (see page 143)

There are only three ingredients in this salad – rocket, zucchini and Parmesan – and they must all be of the very best quality. Choose young zucchini. They must be very fresh, not soft, and should be sliced very thinly at an angle so that they can absorb the flavours of the lemon juice and olive oil.

Stuffed Round Fresh Red Chillies (see page 144)

The chillies used in this recipe come from Piedmont. They are round like small tomatoes and have a mild taste. Never use 'Scotch Bonnet' as they are far too hot for this recipe.

Slow-Cooked Fennel (see page 145)

The Florence fennel season starts just before Christmas; the best bulbs are round and fat with long green stalks. Use the bulbs raw for salads when they are small and young. In this recipe, the flavour changes as the fennel cooks slowly in olive oil, losing its sharp aniseed taste.

Deep-Fried Zucchini (see page 146)

In Italy you might go into a restaurant and have a plate of zucchini fritti while you're waiting for your main course; they also go very well with fish. Choose firm, young zucchini.

Raw Porcini Salad (see page 148)

For this salad you should use small, firm porcini that have only just been picked. They will smell fantastic. Just slice the cleaned porcini and mix with lemon juice, olive oil, salt and pepper. Then toss rocket into this salad so that its pepperiness complements the taste of the raw mushroom. The final ingredient is freshly grated Parmesan, and its saltiness is part of the seasoning of the whole dish.

Swiss Chard with Olive Oil and Lemon (see page 149)

Swiss chard is delicious cooked in this simple way. Varieties to look for and grow include Bright Lights, Ruby Chard and Green Chard. Serve the dish as part of an antipasti di verdura.

Boiled Lemon and Artichoke Heart Salad (see page 150)

This recipe probably originates from Capri but has a North African influence as well.

It is vital that you cook the lemons in a large amount of salted water, otherwise the lemons will taste like marmalade; salt counteracts the acidity of the lemon, and gives it a fresh and very particular taste that complements the boiled artichoke hearts. The slivered almonds add texture, and honey is necessary to sweeten the lemon.

Bruschetta with Garlic and Extra Virgin Olive Oil

6 slices pugliese or other
  sourdough bread, cut 1 cm
  (1/2 in) thick
1 large garlic clove, peeled
extra virgin olive oil

For six

Toast the bread on both sides, then lightly rub with a cut clove of garlic. Drizzle with extra virgin olive oil.

Bruschetta with Squashed Tomatoes, Dried Oregano and Chilli

6 slices sourdough bread
1 garlic clove, peeled
8 ripe, full flavoured, fleshy
  tomatoes
Maldon salt and coarsely ground
  black pepper
1 tablespoon dried oregano
2 small dried chillies
extra virgin olive oil

For six

Toast the bread on both sides, then rub lightly with a cut clove of garlic. Break the tomatoes open and push the tomato flesh roughly into the hot bruschetta. Discard the skin and tough parts of the tomato.

Season generously with salt and pepper, the dried oregano and dried chilli. Pour over a generous amount of extra virgin olive oil and serve.

Bruschetta with Baked Borlotti Beans

2 kg (4.1/2 lb) fresh borlotti
   beans, podded
1 whole bulb garlic, with its skin
   on
2 large tomatoes
1/2 head celery, tops cut off and
   cleaned
olive oil
Maldon salt and freshly ground
   black pepper
6 slices sourdough bruschetta
   (see page 132)

Preheat the oven to
   200°C/400°F/Gas 6.

For six

Place the beans in a porcelain dish (this is better than metal). Add the whole bulb of garlic, the tomatoes, the celery and enough cold water to cover the beans by 1 cm (1/2 in).

Pour enough olive oil into the dish to cover the surface of the water. Cover tightly with foil and pierce to allow the steam to get out. Cook in the oven for 40-60 minutes. When cooked, remove the foil, the garlic, tomato and celery, and season with salt and pepper.

Prepare the bruschetta as described on page 132, and mound the beans on top. Serve immediately.

Bruschetta with Mashed Broad Beans

1.3 kg (3 lb) young broad beans
   (podded weight)
2 garlic cloves, peeled
4 tablespoons fresh mint leaves
4 tablespoons freshly grated
   Pecorino cheese
4 tablespoons olive oil
Maldon salt and freshly ground
   black pepper
juice of 1 lemon
6 slices sourdough bruschetta
   (see page 132)

For six

Pound the broad beans in a pestle and mortar with the garlic and mint. When the mixture is thick in texture, remove and place in a bowl. Stir in the Pecorino and the olive oil. Season with salt and pepper and the lemon juice. Prepare the bruschetta as described on page 132, and serve with the beans.

Bruschetta with Fresh Porcini

1.5 kg (3.1/4 lb) fresh porcini
extra virgin olive oil
4-5 garlic cloves, peeled and
   finely chopped
1/2 bunch fresh flat-leaf parsley,
   leaves picked from stalks and
   roughly chopped
Maldon salt and freshly ground
   black pepper
1 lemon
6 slices sourdough bruschetta
   (see page 132)

For six

Clean the porcini of any dirt or grit using a pastry brush or a damp cloth. Trim the stems with a small knife and slice the porcini through the cap and stem so as to retain the profile.

Heat 3 tablespoons of olive oil in a large frying pan. Add the garlic and gently colour, then add the slices of porcini. Turn up the heat and cook, turning the mushrooms with the garlic. As soon as the porcini are soft add the chopped parsley and season with salt and pepper. Squeeze in the juice of 1 lemon and stir. Prepare the bruschetta as described on page 132 and serve with the mushrooms.

Bruschetta with Cima di Rape

150 g (5 oz) Castellucio lentils or
    lentilles du Puy
3 garlic cloves, peeled
1 sprig fresh sage
Maldon salt and coarsely ground
    black pepper
new season hot and peppery
    extra virgin olive oil
1.5 kg (3.1/4 lb) cima di rape (or
    sprouting broccoli), tough
    stalks removed
juice of 1 lemon
6 slices sourdough bruschetta
    (see page 132)

For four

Wash the lentils and place in a saucepan. Cover with cold water, add 2 of the garlic cloves and the sage and bring to the boil. Lower the heat and simmer gently for 20 minutes or until al dente. Drain and discard the garlic and sage. Season generously with salt and pepper and a generous amount of olive oil. Keep warm.

Wash the cima di rape and discard the tough stalk and yellow leaves. Keep the flowering heads. Blanch in boiling salted water for 5 minutes, drain and lay out to cool.

Prepare the bruschetta as described on page 132, rub with garlic and drizzle with some of the new olive oil.

Toss the cooled cima di rape with the lemon juice, olive oil, and salt and pepper. Place the cima di rape on the bruschetta and scatter with the warm lentils. Serve with prosciutto or salami.

Wood-Roasted Cherry Vine Tomatoes

1.5 kg (3.1/4 lb) cherry tomatoes, on the vine, in about 10 small clusters

3 tablespoons olive oil

1 bunch fresh thyme, in small sprigs

3 garlic cloves, peeled and thinly sliced

Maldon salt and freshly ground black pepper

Preheat the oven to 200°C/400°F/Gas 6.

For four

Place the tomatoes in an oiled roasting pan. Scatter with the thyme and garlic. Drizzle with oil, and season. Roast for 20 minutes.

Wood-Roasted Asparagus

1.6 kg (3.1/4 / 3.1/2 lb) asparagus

olive oil

1 bunch fresh basil, leaves picked from their stalks, roughly chopped

Maldon sea salt and freshly ground black pepper

1 garlic clove, finely chopped

100g (4 oz) stoned Niçoise olives

Preheat the oven to 220°C/425°F/Gas 7.

For four

Trim the asparagus of any woody stalks by gently flexing the base of the stem until it snaps. Discard the woody ends, and wash the green stalks and tips. Dry well and place in a mixing bowl. Toss with enough olive oil to lightly coat each stalk. Add the basil, salt, pepper and garlic, and gently mix.

Arrange in an oiled roasting pan and season again. Add the olives. Roast in the preheated oven for about 10 minutes or until the stalks are wilted and light gold in colour.

Wood-Roasted Peppers

3 red peppers
3 yellow peppers
Maldon salt and freshly ground
    black pepper
3 garlic cloves, peeled and
    chopped
1 bunch dried wild oregano
    (ideally with wild flowers)
extra virgin olive oil

Preheat the oven to
    220°C/425°F/Gas 7.

For four

Slice the peppers in half lengthways and remove the stem, the seeds and any pith. Turn the peppers over and cut into quarters following the natural grooves in the peppers.

Place cut side up in a baking tray, season with salt and pepper and the chopped garlic. Sprinkle the wild oregano inside the peppers and drizzle lightly with olive oil. Bake in the preheated oven for about 45-60 minutes.

Wood-Roasted Zucchini

18 small zucchini
4 garlic cloves, chopped
Maldon salt and freshly ground
    black pepper
extra virgin olive oil

Preheat the oven to
    220°C/425°F/Gas 7.

For six

Pound the garlic and a generous pinch of salt together in a pestle and mortar until you have a paste. Add olive oil until you have a smooth consistency.

Trim the ends of the zucchini to where the seeds start, cut in half lengthways and arrange cut side up on a baking tray. Smear the garlic and oil paste over each of the zucchini with your hands. Sprinkle the black pepper over them – you will not need salt at this stage as it is already in the paste. Bake in the preheated oven for 20 minutes.

Wood-Roasted Pumpkin

2 onion squash, approximately 1
   kg (2.1/4 lb) in weight, peeled
   and cut into 2 cm (3/4 in)
   wedges
150 ml (5 fl oz) olive oil
1 small dried red chilli, crumbled
Maldon salt and freshly ground
   black pepper

For six

Preheat the oven to 240°C/400°F/Gas 6.

Cut the squash in half and then each half into eighths,
2-3 cm (1.1/4-3.1/4 in) wide at the centre. Use a dessert
spoon and scrape away the seeds and coarse fibre.

Place the pieces in an oiled baking dish, season and
drizzle with oil, roast for 30 minutes.

Wood-Roasted Celeriac

2 celeriac, approximately 450 g (1
   lb) each in weight, peeled and
   cut into 2 cm (3/4 in) wedges
1 small bunch fresh thyme, leaves
   picked from the stalks
100 ml (3.1/2 fl oz) olive oil
1 head garlic, separated into
   cloves, peeled and chopped
Maldon salt and freshly ground
   black pepper

For six

Preheat the oven to 220°C/425°F/Gas 7.

Put the celeriac in a bowl with the thyme, garlic, salt,
pepper and olive oil. Mix thoroughly. Place in an oiled
baking dish and cover loosely with foil. Bake for 10
minutes. Remove the foil, turn the pieces over and
roast for 20 minutes.

Wood-Roasted Potato and Trevise

1.5 kg (3 lb) waxy potatoes
   (preferably Roseval), peeled
6 heads trevise
3 tablespoons olive oil
100 g (4 oz) pancetta, thinly
   sliced
3 garlic cloves, peeled and
   chopped
20 sage leaves
Maldon salt and freshly ground
   black pepper
2 tablespoons freshly grated
   Parmesan

For six

Preheat the oven to 180°C/350°F/Gas 4.

Heat 1 tablespoon of the olive oil in a frying pan and fry the pancetta lightly. Add the garlic and sage for a minute, then remove the pan from the heat.

Cut the potatoes lengthways into 5 mm (1/4 in) slices and put into cold water to soak off the starch.

Prepare the trevise by cutting each head lengthways into two. Chop them roughly. Season and add 2 tablespoons of olive oil.

Drain the potatoes and dry. Place the potatoes in a baking dish, and toss with some salt and pepper. Add the pancetta, sage and trevise and the remaining olive oil, and toss again. Cover the baking dish with foil and cook in the oven for 30 minutes.

Remove the foil, sprinkle the vegetables with Parmesan, and return to the oven to brown for 5 minutes.

Wood-Roasted Jerusalem Artichokes

20 Jerusalem artichokes, peeled
100 ml (3.1/2 fl oz) olive oil
1 small bunch fresh thyme, leaves
   picked from the stalks
3 garlic cloves, peeled and finely
   chopped
Maldon salt and freshly ground
   black pepper

For six

Preheat the oven to 220°C/425°F/Gas 7.

Put the artichokes in a bowl with the other ingredients. Mix thoroughly. Place in an oiled baking dish and roast for about 25 minutes, turning over occasionally.

Raw Zucchini Salad

1 kg (2.1/4 lb) young yellow and
   green zucchini
225 g (8 oz) rocket
3 tablespoons extra virgin olive
   oil
juice of 1 lemon
Maldon salt and freshly ground
   black pepper
100-175 g (4-6 oz) Parmesan in
   the piece, sliced into slivers

For four

Trim the ends off the zucchini and slice at an angle into thin rounds. Place in a bowl.

Pick through the rocket, discarding any yellow leaves. Snap off the stalks, then wash and dry the leaves thoroughly.

Mix together the olive oil, lemon juice and salt and pepper, and pour over the zucchini. Mix, then leave to marinate for 5 minutes. Season with salt and pepper.

Divide the rocket leaves between the serving plates. Put the zucchini on top, and then the Parmesan slivers. Add a small amount of freshly ground black pepper, and serve.

Stuffed Round Fresh Red Chillies

12 round red chillies, the size of
  cherry tomatoes
olive oil to cover
6 salted anchovy fillets, rinsed
2 tablespoons salted capers,
  rinsed
2 tablespoons chopped fresh flat-
  leaf parsley
2 tablespoons red wine vinegar

For six

Cut the stems and tops off the chillies to form little cups. Remove the seeds and pith with a small teaspoon (or the end of a spoon). Place the chillies in a small saucepan, just cover with olive oil and bring slowly up to the boil. Remove from the heat and cool.

Chop together the anchovies, capers, and parsley. Stuff each chilli full, shake a few drops of vinegar on to each and serve as part of an antipasti.

Slow-Cooked Fennel

10 fennel bulbs, cut into eighths
5 tablespoons olive oil
Maldon salt and freshly ground
   black pepper
6 garlic cloves, peeled

For six

Heat the oil in a large saucepan. Add the fennel, salt and pepper and cook over a medium heat, stirring occasionally until the fennel begins to brown. This will take about 20 minutes. Add the garlic and continue to fry until the garlic is coloured light brown.

Add 2-3 ladlefuls of boiling water to the fennel, then lower the heat. Simmer gently until the fennel is soft, stirring to prevent sticking. This should take 15 minutes. Check the liquid occasionally; add a little more water if necessary, but there should be no liquid at all when the fennel is cooked.

Deep-Fried Zucchini

For the batter
225 g (8 oz) plain flour
4 tablespoons extra virgin olive
   oil
approximately 300 ml (10 fl oz)
   warm water
4 large egg whites
Maldon salt and freshly ground
   black pepper

For the zucchini chips
24 zucchini, washed, trimmed and
   cut lengthways into quarters
Maldon salt and freshly ground
   black pepper
sunflower oil for deep-frying
3 lemons, cut in half

For six

Make the batter first. Sieve the flour into a large bowl. Pour the olive oil into a well in the centre and slowly stir with a wooden spoon to combine the flour and oil. Slowly add the warm water, little by little, stirring until the batter is the consistency of double cream. Season with salt and pepper and let stand in the fridge for 2 hours.

If the zucchini are large, you may need to trim the seeds and the soft white pulp from the centre.

Heat the sunflower oil in a wide, deep saucepan to a temperature of 180°C/350°F/Gas 4.

Just before cooking, beat the egg whites until stiff and fold into the batter. Dip the zucchini into the batter so they are thinly coated. Tap the zucchini against the side of the bowl to get rid of any excess batter, and place in the hot oil. Fry until they are brown on each side. Drain on kitchen paper and season.

Serve with the lemon halves.

Raw Porcini Salad

1 kg (2.1/4 lb) firm fresh porcini,
  with stalks attached
300 g (10 oz) rocket leaves
Maldon salt and coarsely ground
  black pepper
3 lemons
extra virgin olive oil
200 g (7 oz) Parmesan in the
  piece

For four

Carefully brush clean the mushrooms, removing any sand or grit. Wipe the caps with a damp cloth to remove any earth, and trim the stalks of any rough stems or eaten bits. Using a small sharp knife, slice the porcini lengthways into very thin slices, through the cap and stalk wherever possible.

Wash and dry the rocket leaves. Divide the leaves between the serving plates, cover with the sliced porcini and season first with salt and then with pepper. Squeeze over the juice of half a lemon per plate and then generously drizzle with extra virgin olive oil.

Finally cover each salad with shaved slices of Parmesan.

Swiss Chard with Olive Oil and Lemon

1 kg (2.1/4 lb) Swiss chard
   (weight including stalks)
Maldon salt and coarsely ground
   black pepper
2 lemons
extra virgin olive oil

For four

Pick through the chard leaves and trim the stalks down to the crisp white part. Cut the stalks lengthways into halves if they are more than 3 cm (1.1/2 in) wide. Wash thoroughly and blanch for 8 minutes in boiling salted water. Drain and lay out to cool.

If the leaves are very large (some varieties have leaves as big as serving plates), cut into three. Place the cool chard in a bowl and season generously with salt and pepper. Pour over the lemon juice and extra virgin olive oil.

Boiled Lemon and Artichoke Heart Salad

4 thick-skinned organic lemons

6 small or 4 large artichokes, with stems

Maldon salt and freshly ground black pepper

150 g (5 oz) shelled almonds, toasted

4 tablespoons soft raw honey

juice of 2 lemons

120 ml (4 fl oz) extra virgin olive oil

2 tablespoons fresh thyme leaves

For six

Wash the lemons thoroughly, and put 3 of them whole into a small saucepan. Cover with water and add 100 g (4 oz) salt. Cover with the lid turned upside down so that the handle keeps the lemons below the surface of the water; otherwise the lemons will float and not cook properly. Boil for 20 minutes. The lemons will become soft; the skin should easily be pierced with a fork. Drain and cool.

In boiling salted water, to which you have added the halved remaining lemon, cook the artichokes for 20 minutes or until one of the central leaves will come away with a little give. Drain and cool. Pull away the tough outside leaves, trim the stalks of string and fibre, and cut away the choke if there is any. Cut the hearts into halves, or quarters if they are large. Put in a salad bowl and season with salt and pepper.

Cut the boiled lemons in half and scoop out; discard the pulp and inner segments. Cut the soft skins into quarters and add to the artichoke hearts with the almonds.

Mix the honey with the lemon juice, then add the olive oil. Season and pour over the artichokes. Stir in the thyme.

Sauces

This chapter is about sauces to go with fish and meat, not sauces to go with pasta.

Most of the sauces we make start with the basic ingredients that make up the Italian larder: ie olive oil, salted anchovies, capers, wine vinegars, bread, garlic and a few spices, particularly dried chilli, dried fennel seeds, peppercorns and oregano.

The addition of fresh seasonal herbs that Italians grow, however small their garden or window box, such as basil, flat leaf parsley, rosemary and sage forms the body of these sauces.

Three of the recipes we have chosen are based on a single special ingredient. Red Chilli Sauce that requires large fleshy red chillies; whole grated raw horseradish root for the sauce that famously accompanies Bollito Misto; salted anchovy fillets for Anchovy and Rosemary Sauce.

Fresh Red Chilli Sauce (see page 158)

We make this simple sauce every day to be spooned over char-grilled squid. The bright red, long chillies with thick, juicy flesh have the right heat, not too hot nor too mild.

Horseradish Sauce (see page 158)

Horseradish grows wild all over Europe, and in northern

Italy is used in sauces to accompany Bollito Misto. We learnt this recipe from eating in a restaurant specialising in bollito.

Tarragon Sauce (see page 159)

Like the Horseradish Sauce, this sauce is based on stale bread soaked in wine vinegar – never balsamic as it is too strong. Chopped hard-boiled egg yolks are added to the bread to make the sauce creamy; the tarragon, anchovies and capers are there for the flavour.

Anchovy and Rosemary Sauce (see page 159)

This sauce is simply a combination of salted anchovies and rosemary, lemon juice and olive oil. The anchovies and the rosemary when pounded together give a pungent flavour which is diluted with lemon juice and olive oil. We use the sauce with fish like monkfish and scallops. It's quite sharp, so it complements the sweetness.

Green Sauce (see page 160)

Salsa Verde is a traditional Italian sauce and is usually served with meats; we make our salsa verde thick. We love it with lamb but also with fish.

Use green herbs that are in season. In summer use parsley, basil and mint; in winter just parsley and mint. Add salted anchovies, red wine vinegar, mustard, oil and garlic to make this sauce robust.

Fresh Herb Sauce (see page 160)

This is a sauce we discovered in Florence, and is made with aromatic small-leaf herbs, such as oregano, wild mint, marjoram and fennel. Once again it is made with stale bread, this time soaked in water as well as vinegar, and then mixed with the herbs, capers, anchovies and olive oil, making a wet sauce.

Red Sauce (see page 161)

The red of the recipe can come from peppers alone if they are ripe, or tomatoes and peppers together if made at the end of the summer. In the winter you can use tinned tomatoes and add salted anchovies as well as fresh red chillies to give the sauce strength.

It's delicious with grilled monkfish, any kind of grilled lamb, or with Italian sausages.

Quince Cheese (see page 161)

We use this to melt into the juices of the cooked pheasant to make a simple, gamey sauce.

Fresh Red Chilli Sauce

6 red chillies, seeded and finely
  chopped
25 g (1 oz) fresh flat-leaf parsley,
  chopped
1 garllc clove, peeled and finely
  chopped
Maldon salt and freshly ground
  black pepper
120 ml (4 fl oz) extra virgin olive
  oil

Combine the chillies, parsley and garlic. Season with salt and pepper, and pour the oil over the top.

Horseradish Sauce

1 ciabatta loaf
4 tablespoons red wine vinegar
200 g (7 oz) fresh horseradish,
  peeled
2 garlic cloves, peeled and finely
  chopped
150 ml (5 fl oz) olive oil
Maldon salt and freshly ground
  black pepper

Remove and discard the crust from the bread. Tear the bread into small pieces, then pulse-chop in a food processor to coarse breadcrumbs.

Place the breadcrumbs in a bowl, then add the vinegar and enough water to moisten the breadcrumbs. Put aside for 10 minutes before squeezing as dry as possible.

Finely grate the horseradish on a cheese grater. Combine with the garlic and squeezed breadcrumbs, then slowly add the olive oil, stirring continuously as for mayonnaise. Season with salt and pepper.

Tarragon Sauce

1/2 ciabatta loaf
65 ml (2.1/2 fl oz) red wine
   vinegar
2 hard-boiled egg yolks
100 g (4 oz) fresh tarragon, stalks
   removed, leaves chopped
10 salted anchovy fillets,
   prepared (see page 92) and
   chopped
50 g (2 oz) salted capers,
   prepared (see page 78) and
   chopped
120-175 ml (4-6 fl oz) extra virgin
   olive oil

Tear the bread into small pieces, and soak in the vinegar for 20 minutes. Remove, squeeze dry, and chop, ideally with a mezzaluna.

Mash the egg yolks with a fork.

Very gently combine the bread, tarragon, anchovies, capers and egg in a bowl. Stir in the oil.

Anchovy and Rosemary Sauce

2 tablespoons finely chopped
   fresh rosemary
12 salted anchovy fillets,
   prepared (see page 92)
juice of 2 lemons
150 ml (5 fl oz) extra virgin olive
   oil

Crush the rosemary in a mortar, add the anchovies and pound to a paste. Slowly add the lemon juice, stirring to blend. Finally add the olive oil a drop at a time. When about half has been added, pour in the remainder in a thin, steady stream, stirring continuously. Alternatively, you can use a food processor although this method produces a thicker sauce. Put the rosemary in and chop very finely, then add the anchovy and chop to a thick, fine paste. Pour the oil in slowly. Finally, add the lemon juice.

Green Sauce

1 large bunch fresh flat-leaf
   parsley
1 bunch fresh basil
a handful fresh mint leaves
3 garlic cloves, peeled
100 g (4 oz) salted capers,
   drained and rinsed
100 g (4 oz) anchovies, prepared
   (see page 92)
2 tablespoons red wine vinegar
5 tablespoons olive oil
1 tablespoon Dijon mustard
Maldon salt and freshly ground
   black pepper

Using a food processor, pulse-chop the parsley, basil, mint, garlic, capers and anchovies until roughly blended. (This sauce may be prepared by hand, on a board, preferably using a mezzaluna.)

Transfer to a large bowl and add the vinegar. Slowly pour in the olive oil, stirring constantly, and finally add the mustard. Check for seasoning.

Fresh Herb Sauce

1/2 stale ciabatta or similar loaf
1 tablespoon red wine vinegar
2 garlic cloves, peeled
2 tablespoons salted capers
1 fresh red chilli, seeded
Maldon salt and freshly ground
   black pepper
8 tablespoons mixed wild herbs
   (mint, oregano, marjoram,
   green fennel)
75 ml (2.1/2 fl oz) extra virgin
   olive oil

Soak the bread in the vinegar and 120 ml (4 fl oz) water for 10 minutes. Remove and squeeze out the liquid, and put the bread in a large bowl.

Add the crushed garlic, chopped capers and anchovies, and incorporate into the bread. Add the chilli and season.

Chop a generous amount of each herb and mix into the bread. Slowly pour in the olive oil in a steady stream until the sauce has a rough, thick, bready texture.

Red Sauce

2 fresh red peppers, grilled,
    peeled, seeded and roughly
    chopped
4 ripe tomatoes, skinned, or 1 x
    250 g (8 oz) tin peeled plum
    tomatoes, drained of their
    juices
2 tablespoons olive oil
1 garlic clove, peeled and finely
    chopped
2 fresh red chillies, seeded and
    finely chopped
1 tablespoon dried oregano
Maldon salt and freshly ground
    black pepper
2 small dried chillies, crumbled

Heat the olive oil in a saucepan and gently fry the garlic until it starts to colour. Add the fresh chillies and the oregano. Stir together for one minute. Add the tomatoes and cook for 30 minutes breaking them up as the tomatoes are reduced. Finally add the peppers and cook for a further 10 minutes. Season with salt, pepper and dried chilli.

Quince Cheese

quinces, rubbed to remove down,
    halved if very large
caster sugar
Preheat the oven to
    150°C/300°F/Gas 2

Cover the quinces with foil and bake for about 1.1/2 hours until soft but unbroken.

Cool, halve and remove core. Push through a vegetable mill.

Weigh the pulp and add to an equal amount of caster sugar in a saucepan. Bring to the boil, stirring constantly, until the quince darkens and comes away from the pan sides. This could take up to 30 minutes. Pour on to a large flat cold plate and leave to set.

Puddings

Italian puddings hardly exist, though throughout Italy you come across very interesting regional specialities, like the panforte from Siena or the panettone from Milan. These recipes are often such a closely guarded secret that we decided not to try and make them ourselves but to find out which ones are the best and then buy them from Italy for the restaurant.

Two of the recipes in our series are based on these delicacies. The panforte we chop and marinate in Vin Santo, which is also made around Siena and, in the fashion of flavoured Italian ice creams, we then mix it with our recipe for vanilla ice cream as it is churned.

The panettone bread pudding is made by grilling thick slices, then baking them in custard, making an Italian version of bread and butter pudding.

We still look to the seasons, particularly with our classic almond tart, using strawberries or apricots in the summer, plums or damsons in the autumn, and pears in the winter. It is a delicious and versatile tart using almonds which are a favourite ingredient in Italian puddings.

Another example is the bruschetta with peaches and nectarines. For us, what makes this recipe fit in with our way of cooking is the use of Italian brandy, marinating the fruits to flavour the bruschetta.

We were taught to add grappa to panna cotta by Giuseppe Mazzocolin, an enlightened flavouring for this creamy dessert.

In our Christmas cake, originally devised by Richard Rogers' mother, Dada, all of the crystallised fruits are marinated in rum. It differs from the traditional Christmas cake as there is little flour, lots of chocolate, honey and an enormous amount of nuts. This is also a cake that can be made on Christmas day and eaten right away.

We love making chocolate cakes. In the T.V. programmes we chose to make two of our most popular pure chocolate recipes; both of them use the best quality chocolate and no flour but have very different baking techniques which we hope will excite you and entice you to try them.

Italian sorbets are intensely flavoured. We have included two – a summer one with beautiful, ripe raspberries and lemon, and a winter one with velvety, dark chocolate.

Chocolate Sorbet (see page 170)
This sorbet is a lovely way to enjoy the taste of chocolate. It is fresh, light and easy to make, but relies on the best ingredients, particularly the cocoa powder. Use a French brandy if you can't find Vecchio

Romagna, or some Crème de Cacao, which will intensify the chocolate flavour.

Raspberry Sorbet (see page 170)
Italian fruit sorbets are very simple to make, consisting only of fresh fruit ingredients, thereby retaining an intense flavour. They are usually unstrained.

Panna Cotta with Grappa and Raspberries (see page 172)
This is the Italian version of the cooked creams found in other cuisines, but it is rich, delicious and powerfully flavoured by the grappa. We got the recipe from one of our wine-making friends, who uses his own grappa.

Soften the gelatine by soaking it before you put it in the cream, otherwise you could get lumps. We like to eat panna cotta with raspberries or redcurrants in the summer and caramelised blood oranges in the winter.

Chocolate Nemesis (see page 174)
We make this chocolate cake every day, and it's the most popular dessert in the restaurant. Use the cake tin size specified in the recipe; one with a different depth or circumference will alter the way the cake cooks. The bain-marie must be filled right to the rim with hot water before cooking; leave the cake in the bain-marie to cool down. The cake must be completely cold before you turn it out.

Pressed Chocolate Cake (see page 175)

This cake contains no flour, only butter, eggs, sugar, chocolate and cocoa powder. The cake is made as normal but beaten egg whites are added so that it rises like a soufflé. When it's risen but still moist take it out of the oven, put a plate on top, and press down with weights. The cake slowly squashes down to a dense middle with a crisp, rough edge. It is important not to overcook this cake.

Polenta and Lemon Cake (see page 176)

This is based on a traditional almond and lemon cake of Marcella Hazan's, but we have substituted polenta for the white flour. The cake is very light and simple to make: it's all made in one bowl, there's no separate beating of ingredients. The generous use of lemon complements the richness of the polenta.

Almond Tart with Strawberries (see page 178)

The basic recipe for almond tart has been on the menu at the River Cafe since the day it started. It was originally made with pears, cooked in the almond filling. In the summer, the tart is baked first, then strawberries or raspberries are scattered on top.

The pastry technique – grating it rather than rolling it – was introduced to us by one of our young chefs. It's a fantastic way of doing it, as it is handled as little as possible.

Almond, Orange, Lemon and Whisky Cake (see page 179)

This is an unusual cake. The ground almonds which are added to the cake make it moist; soaking it in the orange, lemon and whisky syrup gives it an intense aroma and lovely flavour.

Dada's Christmas Cake (see page 180)

This recipe was devised by Dada Rogers, an Italian who moved to London during the war. She started out making a cross between English Christmas cake and Italian panforte, but over some 35 years she slowly changed the recipe. She would decrease the flour, increase the chocolate, decrease the butter, and increase the fruit.

The ingredients in this cake are very important, and must be of the very best quality. Everything must be chopped by hand, not in the processor, as nothing in this cake is smooth and refined. It can be made in different sizes and given as presents, and it keeps well.

Panettone Bread Pudding (see page 181)

We have taken the traditional British bread and butter pudding, and Italianised it. It uses panettone, an Italian Christmas cake-bread which is made with yeast and lots of butter. By toasting it, you give the pudding another flavour.

Panforte Ice-Cream (see page 182)

Panforte comes from Siena, and it's a very rich Christmas confection, made with nuts, honey, citrus peel and spices. Icing sugar is pressed into the top. It has a texture like nougat. Vin Santo is made in the same area of Italy and is used to marinate the panforte.

Monte Bianco (see page 184)

This recipe comes from Le Marche where there are a lot of chestnut woods. Fresh chestnuts have to be blanched and then kept hot in order to take the peel and then the inner skin off. Pipe into a mountain shape on a large plate and cover with shaved chocolate.

Bruschetta with Summer Fruits (see page 185)

Use sourdough bread as you want one that is able to absorb the fruit juices but keep its shape. Use firm summer fruits such as peaches or nectarines, not berries which will collapse in the oven. Marinating the fruits in the vanilla-flavoured sugar and alcohol is an important part of the recipe.

Chocolate Sorbet

750 ml (generous 1.1/4 pints)
    water
250 g (9 oz) caster sugar
150 g (5 oz) cocoa powder
100 ml (3.1/2 fl oz) Vecchio
    Romagna (Italian brandy)

For six

Gently boil the water and sugar together to dissolve the sugar, about 4 minutes. To this light syrup you then add the cocoa powder. Cook gently, stirring from time to time for 15-20 minutes until the cocoa powder is completely dissolved. Strain, cool and then add the brandy.

Put the mixture into an ice-cream maker, and churn until frozen, or freeze in flat freezer trays, stirring every now and again to break up the crystals until solid. This will take up to 1.1/2 hours.

Raspberry Sorbet

800 g (1.3/4 lb) fresh ripe
    raspberries
1 whole thick-skinned organic
    lemon, washed
350-400 g (12-14 oz) caster sugar
    (depending on how sweet the
    raspberries are)
juice of 1/2-1 lemon

For six

Cut the whole lemon into 1 cm (1/2 in) pieces, and remove any pips. Put the pieces into a food processor with the caster sugar and blend until the lemon and sugar have combined to a thick purée: little pieces of lemon skin should still be visible. Add the raspberries, and continue to blend until combined. Add the juice of 1/2 lemon, taste and add more if necessary. The lemon flavour should be intense but should not overpower the raspberries.

Pour into an ice-cream maker and churn for 20 minutes. Remove and put in a freezer and allow to get stiffer before serving. Alternatively pour the mixture into flat freezing trays and freeze – stirring to break the crystals every half hour – until solid. This will take about 1.1/2 hours.

Panna Cotta with Grappa and Raspberries

1.2 litres (2 pints) double cream
2 vanilla pods
thinly pared rind of 2 lemons
3 gelatine leaves
150 ml (5 fl oz) cold milk
150 g (5 oz) icing sugar
120 ml (4 fl oz) grappa, plus
   extra to serve
3 punnets raspberries

For six

Pour 900 ml (1.1/2 pints) of the cream into a pan, add the vanilla pods and lemon rind, bring to the boil, then simmer until reduced by about one-third. Remove the cooked lemon rind and keep to one side. Remove the vanilla pods and scrape the softened insides into the cream.

Soak the gelatine in the milk for about 15 minutes or until soft. Remove the gelatine, heat the milk until boiling, then return the gelatine to the milk and stir until dissolved. Pour the milk and gelatine mixture into the hot cream through a sieve, stir, then leave to cool.

Lightly whip the remaining cream with the icing sugar, fold into the cooled cooked cream, then add the grappa. Place a piece of cooked lemon rind in each of six small 200 ml (7 fl oz) moulds or bowls, pour in the cream mixture and allow to set in the fridge for at least 2 hours.

Turn out on to dessert plates and serve with fresh raspberries and a tablespoon of extra grappa poured over the top.

Chocolate Nemesis

675 g (1.1/2 lb) bitter-sweet
   chocolate, broken into small
   pieces
10 whole eggs
575 g (1 lb 5 oz) caster sugar
450 g (1 lb) unsalted butter,
   softened

For ten to twelve

Preheat the oven to 160°C/325°F/Gas 3.

Line a 30 x 5 cm (12 x 2 in) cake tin with greaseproof paper, then grease and flour it.

Beat the eggs with one-third of the sugar until the volume quadruples – this will take at least 10 minutes with an electric mixer.

Heat the remaining sugar in a small pan with 250 ml (8 fl oz) water until the sugar has dissolved to a syrup.

Place the chocolate and butter in the hot syrup and stir to combine. Remove from the heat and allow to cool slightly.

Add the warm chocolate syrup to the eggs and continue to beat, rather more gently, until completely combined – about 20 seconds, no more. Pour into the cake tin and place in a bain-marie of hot water. It is essential, if the cake is to cook evenly, that the water is hot and that it comes up to the rim of the tin. Bake in the preheated oven for 40 minutes to 1 hour or until set. Test by placing the flat of your hand gently on the surface. The cake should feel just set *not* firm like a baked cake.

Leave to become completely cold in the tin before turning out.

Pressed Chocolate Cake

400 g (14 oz) best-quality bitter-
   sweet chocolate, broken into
   pieces
300 g (10 oz) unsalted butter
10 eggs, separated
225 g (8 oz) caster sugar
4 tablespoons the best quality
   cocoa powder

For ten

Preheat the oven to 180°C/350°F/Gas 4.

Butter and flour a 30 x 7.5 cm (12 x 3 in) cake tin.

Melt the chocolate with the butter in a bowl over a pan of simmering water – the water should not be allowed to touch the bowl. Remove the bowl from the pan, cool a little. Whisk the egg yolks with the sugar until pale and thick. Stir gently into the cooled chocolate mixture. Finally fold in the cocoa powder.

Beat the egg whites until they form soft peaks. Fold into the chocolate mixture, one-third at a time.

Pour the mixture into the prepared cake tin and bake in the oven for approximately 30 minutes or until the cake has risen like a soufflé and is slightly set.

Now place on top a plate that fits within a centimetre inside the tin rim. Press down firmly, and put a weight on top of it to squash the cake and allow the edges to erupt over the edge. Allow to cool before turning out.

Polenta and Lemon Cake

450 g (1 lb) unsalted butter,
  softened
450 g (1 lb) caster sugar
450 g (1 lb) ground almonds
2 teaspoons good vanilla essence
6 eggs
zest of 4 lemons
juice of 1 lemon
225 g (8 oz) polenta flour
1.1/2 teaspoons baking powder
1/4 teaspoon salt

For ten

Preheat the oven to 160°C/325°F/Gas 3.

Butter and flour a 30 cm (12 in) cake tin.

Beat the butter and sugar together until pale and light. Stir in the ground almonds and vanilla. Beat in the eggs, one at a time. Fold in the lemon zest and lemon juice, the polenta, baking powder and salt.

Spoon into the prepared tin and bake in the preheated oven for 45-50 minutes or until set. The cake will not rise and should be lightly browned on top.

Almond Tart with Strawberries

For the sweet pastry
350 g (12 oz) plain flour
a pinch of salt
225 g (8 oz) unsalted cold butter,
    cut into cubes
100 g (4 oz) icing sugar
3 organic egg yolks

For the filling
350 g (12 oz) unsalted butter,
    softened
350 g (12 oz) caster sugar
350 g (12 oz) blanched whole
    almonds
4 organic eggs

To decorate
2 punnets strawberries
icing sugar, for dusting

For ten to twelve

For the sweet pastry, pulse the flour, salt and butter in a food processor until the mixture resembles coarse breadcrumbs. Add the sugar then the egg yolks and pulse. The mixture will immediately combine and leave the sides of the bowl. Remove, wrap in cling film, and chill for at least 1 hour.

Preheat the oven to 180°C/350°F/Gas 4.

Coarsely grate the pastry into a 30 cm (12 in) loose-bottomed fluted flan tin, then press it evenly on to the sides and base, using the ball of your hand. Do this as quickly as possible. Bake blind for 20 minutes until very light brown. Cool. Reduce the oven temperature to 150°C/300°F/Gas 2.

For the filling, cream the butter and sugar until the mixture is pale and light. Put the almonds in a food processor and chop until fine. Add the butter and sugar and blend, then beat in the eggs one by one. Pour into the pastry case and bake for 40 minutes. Cool.

Hull the strawberries and cut them into wedges. Stick these into the top of the tart so that they stand upright, slanting in the middle. When completely covered, dust with icing sugar and serve.

Almond, Orange, Lemon and Whisky Cake

8 large free-range eggs, separated
200 g (7 oz) caster sugar
zest of 2 washed oranges
zest of 2 washed lemons
300 g (10 oz) blanched almonds,
    finely ground

For the syrup
juice of 3 oranges, approximately
    320 ml (10.1/2 fl oz)
juice of 4 lemons, approximately
    320 ml (10.1/2 fl oz)
75 g (3 oz) caster sugar
1 cinnamon stick
500 ml (17 fl oz) whisky

To serve
crème fraîche or mascarpone

For eight

Preheat the oven to 180°C/350°F/Gas 4.

Butter and line a 26 x 26 x 5 cm (10.1/2 x 10.1/2 x 2 in) cake tin with baking parchment.

Beat the egg yolks with the sugar until pale, add the citrus zests and ground almonds, and stir together briefly. Beat the egg whites to soft peaks and fold into the almond and egg yolk mixture. Pour into the cake tin and bake in the oven for 35-45 minutes until set.

Make the syrup by heating the orange and lemon juice with the sugar and cinnamon in a pan over a moderate heat until reduced a little, then add the whisky.

When the cake is cooked and still hot, prick the whole surface with a pointed knife and pour over the syrup. Make sure all the liquid has soaked into the cake.

Remove the cake from the tin when completely cooled. Serve with crème fraîche or mascarpone.

Dada's Christmas Cake

250 g (9 oz) unsalted butter, softened, plus a little for the tin

100 g (4 oz) glacé cherries (not artificially coloured)

50 g (2 oz) angelica

350 g (12 oz) candied mixed lemon and orange peel

750 ml (26 fl oz) dark rum

100 g (4 oz) whole shelled hazelnuts

100 g (4 oz) chopped shelled hazelnuts

150 g (5 oz) blanched whole almonds

150 g (5 oz) unblanched whole almonds

350 g (12 oz) ground almonds

100 g (4 oz) caster sugar

220 g (8 oz) plain flour

5 organic eggs

3 unwaxed organic lemons

500 g (1 lb 2 oz) honey

250 g (9 oz) apricot jam

150 g (5 oz) raisins

650 g (1 lb 7 oz) bitter-sweet chocolate, chopped

For eight

Preheat the oven to 140°C/275°F/Gas 1.

Butter a 30 x 5 cm (12 x 2 in) cake tin and line the bottom with baking parchment. Chop the cherries, angelica, candied orange and lemon peel and marinate for a minimum of 1 hour in 350 ml (12 fl oz) of the rum.

Roast the hazelnuts and blanched almonds until brown. Peel and chop half of the hazelnuts and all of the roasted blanched almonds roughly. Roughly chop half of the unblanched almonds and flaked almonds. Mix together with all of the unchopped nuts except the ground almonds.

Cream the remaining butter and the sugar together until pale. Sift in the flour, then add the eggs one at a time. Add 100 g (4 oz) of the ground almonds and mix.

Peel the lemons and dice the peel roughly. Drain the marinated fruit (reserving the rum), and mix in the lemon peel, honey and apricot jam.

In a large bowl combine the butter and sugar mixture with all the fruit and nuts, as well as the rest of the ground almonds and the chocolate. Add the remaining rum as well as that from the fruit. Pour into the tin.

Reduce the temperature to 110°C/225°F/Gas 1/4 and bake for 30 minutes.

Panettone Bread Pudding

1 panettone 2 kg (4 lb 2 oz), cut
  into 1 cm (1/2 in) slices
a little butter for the dish
500 ml (17 fl oz) milk
500 ml (17 fl oz) double cream
4 large eggs
120 g (4.1/2 oz) caster sugar

For eight

Preheat the oven to 150°C/300°F/Gas 2.

Lightly grill each slice of the panettone on both sides. Butter a shallow oval baking dish and carefully arrange the panettone slices, slightly overlapping, to fill the dish.

Mix the milk and cream together, and slowly bring to the boil. Beat the eggs with the sugar until light, and then carefully add the hot milk mixture.

Pour the hot custard over the panettone slices. Push the slices down so that each is just covered by the custard. Sit for a while to allow the slices to absorb the liquid.

Place the baking dish in a bain-marie in the preheated oven and bake for 45-60 minutes. The custard should be just set. Serve warm.

Panforte Ice-Cream

500 g (5 oz) panforte di Siena
150 ml (5 fl oz) Vin Santo
900 ml (1.1/2 pints) double cream
225 ml (7.1/2 fl oz) milk
2 vanilla pods
8 organic egg yolks
175 g (6 oz) caster sugar

For six

Chop three-quarters of the panforte into small pieces in a food processor or by hand. Place in a bowl and pour over the Vin Santo.

In a thick-bottomed saucepan, combine the cream and milk. Using a knife, scrape the vanilla seeds out of the pods into the mixture. Gently heat until the mixture almost reaches boiling point.

Beat the egg yolks and sugar together until pale and thick. Pour a little of the hot cream mixture into the egg yolks and stir. Return this mixture to the remainder of the hot cream and stir over a low heat, cooking it very gently. The mixture will gradually thicken, but do not allow it to boil. At this point remove from the heat, pour into a bowl and allow to cool.

When cool, stir in the panforte mixture. Pour into an ice-cream maker and churn until frozen, or freeze in a suitable container, stirring every now and again. Serve with a thin wedge of the remaining panforte.

Monte Bianco

1 kg (2.1/4 lb) fresh chestnuts
1 litre (1.3/4 pints) milk
100 g (4 oz) caster sugar
2 vanilla pods, split open and
   seeds loosened
250 g (9 oz) crème fraîche
a little good-quality bitter
   chocolate

For six

Bring a large saucepan of water to the boil.

Using a small knife, score the fresh chestnuts across the base of the shells. Put them into cold water, bring to the boil and cook for 15-20 minutes according to size. Remove a few chestnuts at a time to shell them; the shell will come off easily so long as the chestnuts are kept hot in the cooking water (or in a tea-towel dipped in boiling water). Squeeze each chestnut to crack the shell open, then prise the nuts out of the shell. Carefully remove the bitter inner skin.

Heat the milk in a large pan, add the sugar, split vanilla pods and the shelled and skinned chestnuts, and simmer gently for 40 minutes until the chestnuts become quite soft; the liquid will have reduced.

Put the cooked chestnuts through a coarse mouli or sieve. Add enough of the remaining reduced milk to bring the mixture together to form a thick dough. Test for sweetness, then spoon into a piping bag with a small plain nozzle. Pipe the chestnut dough out into a mountain shape on a flat serving plate; this will take some time!

Serve with crème fraîche and bitter chocolate grated on top.

Bruschetta with Summer Fruits

6 apricots

6 very ripe nectarines or white
   peaches

6 plums

6 slices sourdough bread, cut 1.5
   cm (1/2 in) thick with bottom
   crusts removed

100 g (4 oz) unsalted butter,
   softened

2 vanilla pods

250 g (9 oz) caster sugar

50 ml (2 fl oz) Vecchio Romagna
   (Italian brandy) or Amaretto
   (almond liqueur)

crème fraîche to serve

For six

Preheat the oven to 200°C/400°F/Gas 6.

Butter a baking tray. Butter each slice of bread on one side only.

Cut the vanilla pods into small pieces, and pound with the sugar in a mortar. Alternatively, roughly chop the vanilla with the sugar in a food processor.

Halve the fruits and remove the stones. Put the fruits together in a bowl. Stir in the vanilla sugar and the alcohol. Leave to marinate for 20 minutes or so.

Break and press two halves of nectarine, cut side down, on to each slice of buttered bread so that it absorbs the juices. Place two halves of apricots and plums, cut side up, on top of each slice, and pour over the remaining juices from the bowl.

Place in a baking tray and bake in the preheated oven for 20-25 minutes. They should be crisp on the edges and the fruits cooked. Serve warm with crème fraîche.

Index

Index

Index

Index

Index

Acknowledgements:

Savannah Alvarez
Violet Alvarez
Vashti Armit
Karl Bjørge
Bepe Camia
Anselmo Chiarli
Mauro Chiarli
Aldo Conterno
Beatrice Contini-Bonacossi
Mike Dowding
John Edwards
Antonio Farina
Isaldo Ferrarese
Susan Fleming
Inger Marie Giethammer
David Gleave
Kevin Graham
Kenneth Gray
Ossie Gray
Celia Harvey
Garry John Hughes
Piero Lanini
David MacIlwaine

Antonio Marella
Bianca Martini
Guiseppe Mazzocolin
Fiona MacIntyre
Grant McKee
Francis McNeil
John Meis
Luciano Michele
Paul Murray
Famiglia Nanini
Clive Osborne
Sue Osborne
Jean Pigozzi
Paolo Pomposi
Patrizio Pomposi
Arthur Potts-Dawson
Theo Randall
Ab Rogers
Richard Rogers
Zad Rogers
Renzo Sobrino
Sarah Spencer
Marchesi Franca Spinola
Ben Warwick